Revelation Abridged

Revelation Abridged

Commentary Improving Daily Life

Paul Brown

RESOURCE *Publications* • Eugene, Oregon

REVELATION ABRIDGED
Commentary Improving Daily Life

Copyright © 2021 Paul Brown. All rights reserved. Except for brief quotations in critical publications or reviews, no part of this book may be reproduced in any manner without prior written permission from the publisher. Write: Permissions, Wipf and Stock Publishers, 199 W. 8th Ave., Suite 3, Eugene, OR 97401.

Resource Publications
An Imprint of Wipf and Stock Publishers
199 W. 8th Ave., Suite 3
Eugene, OR 97401

www.wipfandstock.com

PAPERBACK ISBN: 978-1-7252-9335-9
HARDCOVER ISBN: 978-1-7252-9336-6
EBOOK ISBN: 978-1-7252-9337-3

06/10/21

Contents

List of Figures | xi
Author's Comments | xiii

    I) Highlights with Purpose | xiii
    II) The Arch | xiv
    III) Viewpoint Unique | xv
    IV) Symbols & Qualities | xvi
    V) Counter-Facts | xvii
    VI) Slow or Fast, Every Step is Cause for Rejoicing | xviii
    VII) Supportive Format | xix

Introduction Preview | 2
Introduction (Rev. 1:1—1:18) | 3

    I) Revealing (God, Christ, Spirit, Servants) | 3
    II) Blessing (Study, Contemplate, Practice) | 4
    III) Greeting (Shalom Aleichem; Salaam Alaykum) | 5
    IV) Redemption (Corporeal, Moral, Enlightened) | 6
    V) Creator (Eternal, Almighty) | 7
    VI) Creating (Great Voice) | 8
    VII) Creation (Divine Expression) | 9

Introduction Summation | 10

Letters Preview | 11
Letters (Rev. 1:19—3:22) | 12

    I) Ephesus (Discretion—antediluvian Creation Stories) | 13
    II) Smyrna (Fidelity—patriarchs Joseph/Moses) | 14
    III) Pergamos (Righteousness—prophets Elijah & Elisha) | 15
    IV) Thyatira (Self-Control—kings Saul & David) | 16
    V) Sardis (Vigilance—schism Israel/Judah) | 17
    VI) Philadelphia (Impartiality—returning Remnant) | 18
    VII) Laodicea (Empathy—occupation by Rome) | 19

Letters Summation | 20

Vision One Preview | 22
Vision Seven Preview | 23

*****Vision One**: Holy Tabernacle (Rev. 4:1—5:14) | 24
*****Vision Seven**: Holy City (Rev. 21:9—22:2) | 25

    I) Holy of Holies (Our Father) | 26
    I) City of Cities (Light) | 27

    II) Cherubim (in Heaven) | 28
    II) Precious Clarity (Heaven) | 29

    III) Altar of Incense (Hallowed Name) | 30
    III) Praise & Salvation (Growth & Identity) | 31

    IVa) Lamp's Light (Will Done) | 32
    IVa) Foursquare Order (Universal Order) | 33

    IVb) Four Ensigns (Earth & Heaven) | 34
    IVb) Glory's Light (Universe Coincident) | 35

    V) Showbread (Daily Bread) | 36
    V) Book of Life (Angelic Sustenance) | 37

    VI) Laver of Water (Forgiveness) | 38
    VI) Water of Life (Pure Offspring) | 39

    VII) Altar of Sacrifice (Deliverance) | 40
    VII) Tree of Life (Sanctification) | 41

        (interlude—for thine is the kingdom . . .) | 42
        (interlude—which bare . . .) | 43

Vision One Summation | 44
Vision Seven Summation | 45

Vision Two Preview | 46
Vision Six Preview | 47
***Vision Two**: Seals Removed (Rev. 6:1—8:1) | 48
***Vision Six**: Goodness Sung (Rev. 19:1—21:8) | 49

    I) Horse of Deception vs Unpretentious Ox | 50
    I) Alleluia | 51

    II) Horse of Wrath vs Dignified Lion | 52
    II) Alleluia | 53

    III) Horse of Greed vs Generous Man | 54
    III) Alleluia | 55

    IV) Horse of Pseudo Science vs Perceptive Eagle | 56
    IV) Alleluia | 57

        (interlude—horsemen impotent) | 58
        (interlude—creator omnipotent) | 59

    V) Desertion vs Persistence | 60
    V) Marriage Feast | 61

    VI) Concealment vs Repentance | 62
    VI) True & Faithful | 63

        (interlude—glory for servants) | 64
        (interlude—doom for evildoers) | 65

    VII) All Things Calm | 72
    VII) All Things New | 73

Vision Two Summation | 74
Vision Six Summation | 75

Vision Three Preview | 76
Vision Five Preview | 77

*****Vision Three**: Trumpets of Justice (Rev. 8:2—12:6) | 78
*****Vision Five**: Cups of Mercy (Rev. 15:1—18:24) | 79

    I) Substance without Justice is consumed | 80
    I) Substance without Mercy is grievous | 81

    II) Intelligence without Justice is consumed | 82
    II) Intelligence without Mercy is drowning madness | 83

    III) Experience without Justice is consumed | 84
    III) Experience without Mercy is bitter blood to drink | 85

    IV) Seasons without Justice is consumed | 86
    IV) Seasons without Mercy is great heat | 87

        (interlude—woes) | 88
        (interlude—woes) | 89

    V) Authority without Justice is a woe | 90
    V) Authority without Mercy is a dark pit of pain | 91

    VI) Human Rights without Justice is a woe | 92
    VI) Human Rights without Mercy is genocide | 93

        (interlude—true witnesses) | 94
        (interlude—false witnesses) | 95
        (interlude—true witnesses) | 96
        (interlude—false witnesses) | 97

    VII) Mercy without Justice is a woe | 98
    VII) Justice without Mercy is a plague| 99

        (extension—Virgin) | 100
        (extension—Harlot) | 101

Vision Three Summation | 108
Vision Five Summation | 109

Vision Four Preview | 110
    Dragon—Demonic Falsehoods | 110
    Central Key | 110
    Divine—Angelic Truths | 110
***Vision Four** Keystone (Rev. 12:7—14:20) | 111

Dragon Demons | 112
Divine Angels | 113

    I) Dragon Temporal | 114
    I) Gospel Everlasting | 115

    II) Dragon Persecutes (virgin & child) | 116
    II) Self-Destruction (harlot & offspring) | 117

    III) Dragon Pours (flood of despair) | 118
    III) Inspiration Pours (wine of inspiration) | 119

    IV) Dragon (wroth with servants) | 120
    IV) Remnant (blessed servants) | 121

    V) Beast of Sea (anti-Comforter) | 122
    V) Harvest of Bread (Christ) | 123

    VI) Beast of Earth (anti-Christ) | 124
    VI) Harvest of Wine (Holy Spirit) | 125

    VII) Mark of Sacrilegious | 126
    VII) Winepress of Communion | 127

Central Key | 128
    Father's Mark | 129
    New Song | 130
    Innocent Perfection | 131

Vision Four Summation | 132

Revelation Conclusion | 133
> Postlude (Rev. 22:3—22:5) | 134
> Epilogue (Rev. 22:6—22:14) | 135
> Benediction (Rev. 22:15—22:21) | 135

Seven Visions Summation | 136

Matrix of Innocense & Perfection | 138

Author's Final Thought | 139

List of Figures

Figure-arch | xiv

Figure-intro7 | 10

Figure-letters7 | 11

Figure-v-one | 44

Figure-v-seven | 45

Figure-v-two | 74

Figure-v-six | 75

Figure-justice | 108

Figure-mercy | 109

Figure-v-four | 132

Figure-archsmall | 136

Figure-matrix | 138

Author's Comments

I) Highlights with Purpose

My purpose is to uncomplicate the Book of Revelation like a scientist would do to simplify quantum mechanics for a general audience.

Highlighting a few sacred words from Revelation's seven visions eliminates the need of examining a menagerie of detail. Just these phrases have enough luster to illuminate an indispensable essence—practical means for improving daily life.

This abridged commentary does not talk about doctrinal theories, past/present/future geopolitics, preterist or historicist views, end-of-the-world, or the jubilee. Instead it highlights Revelation's positive activities for experiencing more harmony in every day life.

This book concludes with the key fact that the offspring of God are innocent perfection. If this is true, what of the evil that is so malicious in the world? Answer, Revelation clearly shows that evil destroys itself. Evil thoughts and actions will be self-seen; evident in disharmony, producing suffering upon itself. Sooner or later progress will spring forth; the old mortal means and methods will be discarded for the new immortal cause and effect. Innocent perfection will blossom naturally. *"the desert shall rejoice, and blossom as the rose." (Isaiah 35:1)*.

This abridged commentary does not cover every nuance, so feel free to dig deeper into the details of Revelation—worth the study when one is determined to put forth the effort.

II) The Arch

Scholars have formalized many differing outlines of the Book of Revelation. There are hordes of diverse diagrams and geometric structures. Some focus on very unique schemes, and many provide food for thought.

My approach for outlining the Book of Revelation for this abridged commentary follows the architectural structure of a sevenfold stone arch, the middle stone being called the keystone.

Consider a well-crafted novel's story where there is a beginning, a middle, and an end. Usually the beginning often concerns a particular goal, and the end is often a mirrored transformation of the goal. The novel's middle is a turning point, the catalyst that leavens the whole.

The sides of the arch of the Book of Revelation compliment each other in style and meaning, i.e., vision one to vision seven, and so forth. These sides support the central keystone that marks all God's creation as innocent perfection.

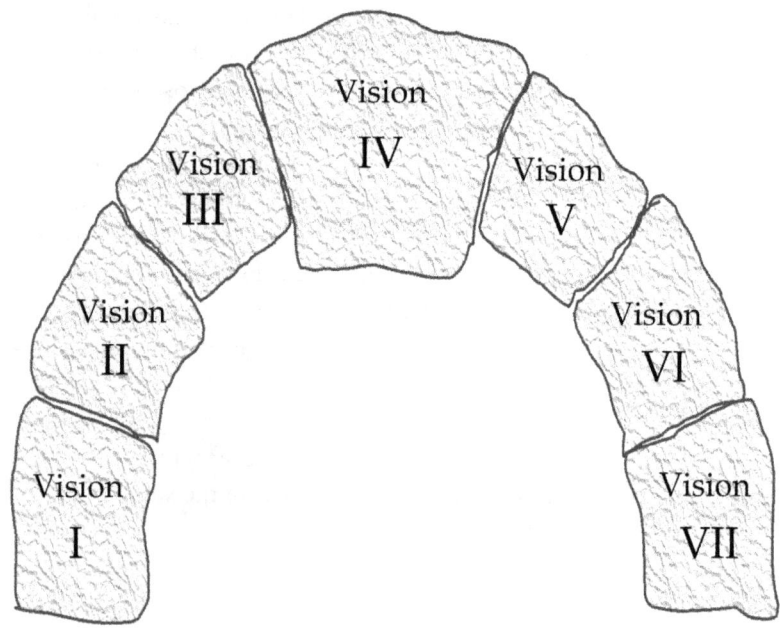

III) Viewpoint Unique

Instead of fearing the chaos in Revelation, discover a fresh viewpoint where only grace pours forth.

My outlook comes from a studied background. Having graduated as an aerospace engineer, and after working for the Navy, I turned my next years to theological study and writing. I became a part-time chaplain for a Christian church. Later I met the requirements and obtained an honorary divinity degree, and am a member of the American School of Oriental Research. I have traveled the Lands of the Bible, and visited historic religious sites across Europe. I love teaching Sunday School, and thoroughly enjoy symbolism, metaphors, etc., and investigating unique scholarly viewpoints. Many of my discoveries have occurred during decades of study.

Let us agree to disagree. Let us rise above the plethora of different faiths and traditions that declare stubborn war upon each other in the name of the one God. Regrettably there is too much disharmony in the world, epitomized by the major religious schisms: Jews of the East vs West, Roman Catholic vs Greek Orthodox, Shiite vs Sunni, Protestant vs Non-Traditionalists. Yet are we not all from the same Father/Mother? To promote the sense of family across all faiths, supportive interfaith quotes are given from the Jewish Tanakh (or other spelling), the Islamic Quran (or other spelling), and the Christian New Testament—finding much agreement between them.

With an uplifting viewpoint more joy and compassion in daily life can overflow toward neighbors and surroundings. Have another interpretation? Great! Revelation is as a flower and many go to describe it: Many roads, one path; many people, one family.

Regarding quotes from the King James Version (KJV) of the Bible; Rights in the Authorized (King James) Version of the Bible are administered in the United Kingdom by the Crown's patentee, Cambridge University Press.

IV) Symbols & Qualities

Symbolism is used throughout Revelation. Yet one can become burdened with literal exactness by taking these symbols as merely physical objects. Instead, approach these prophetic verses like an impressionistic artist. Let us think of qualities that these symbols express: for water the quality of purity or flowing ideas; for a tree the qualities of life, fruition, beauty, etc.

The point is not to merely envision or reproduce medieval or renaissance depictions. For example if a verse denotes an angel, try not to picture a classic painting with a human body flying with bird-like wings. Instead mentally compose a thought image without material form—like an illuminating messenger taking instantaneous flight; the messenger flying above corporeal concerns with incorporeal fresh ideals and comforting grace.

Regarding symbolic numerology, though there appear lots of sequences—four, seven, etc.—such sequences are less important than the inspired ideas they represent.

Transform objects into ideas. Let impressionistic images be mental. Exchange physical forms for metaphysical ideas. Discover metaphors ever-present. Nature overflows with symbols that hint of the infinite attributes of the Divine.

Is there more to human existence than the five senses? *"My kingdom is not of this world:" (John 18:36).* Honor, obedience, honesty, trustworthiness, etc. these invisible qualities are of the spiritual world. These traits are incorporeal; *"the kingdom of God is within you." (Luke 17:21).*

Focusing attention toward fleshly purposes misses the rainbow of spiritual promises; *"love is the fulfilling of the law." (Romans 13:10).*

V) Counter-Facts

The Book of Revelation reveals "the nature of good" and "the nature of evil." Thankfully evil always destroys itself, and is never able to overpower good. The nature of good is the exact opposite of the nature of evil. Thus good is the counter-fact to evil, just like light and darkness are counter-facts, or opposites.

If a verse or passage conveys the idea "evil brings wrath," the opposite then is "good brings kindness." The counter-fact to "evil brings disease" is "good brings health." Woes and afflictions result from evil thought and activity. Benedictions and blessings result from good thought and activity.

As free moral agents our purpose is: To differentiate and separate the evil tares from the good wheat in everyday harvesting (see Matthew 13:24–30). Therefore understanding the concept of counter-facts can bring much harmony to daily life.

Sometimes mortal life seems like a pit, where one is being buried everyday with problems. Well, what is the counter-fact? Remember the donkey-in-the-pit anecdote. While barraged by people throwing dirt on him, the donkey, instead of complaining, shook off the dirt and stood upon it. After much persistence the donkey, not letting the burdens of discouragement weigh him down, eventually rose above the level of the pit. Then with dominion the donkey liberated himself, and never glanced back. Look at the problems Joseph and Job overcame. In faithful devotion, while under great tribulations, they gained glorious benedictions.

While Revelation describes the destruction of unhealthy character traits in thought and deed, it also unveils our salvation through healthful character motives and traits—attainable to the discerning consciousness.

Basic counter-facts turn seeming chaos into announcements of abundant grace for all. *"I will lead them in paths that they have not known: I will make darkness light before them, and crooked things straight." (Isaiah 42:16)*.

VI) Slow or Fast, Every Step is Cause for Rejoicing

One may find Revelation overwhelming because of the amount of evil qualities it uncovers, and perhaps of the amount of good qualities that need to be practiced. However be not overwhelmed. Each advancing step one takes is cause for rejoicing.

Never feel unworthy of God. Never agree with self-destructive miasmas. Consider the following experience extraordinaire. A parent was feeling ill will toward a family member. The parent was saddened that they could not muster much love for the individual. Willing to change thought, the parent opened themselves to listen to the Supreme. Soon an angel message asked, what happens when a young baby takes its first steps? Answer: Adults clap and express great joy. No one condemns or rebukes because as yet the child cannot ride a bike or solve a trigonometry problem. So the parent reasoned: we are all like young children learning as we grow. Thus the expression of love or kindness at this moment may only be a small baby step. Yet God is figuratively clapping and rejoicing for every step ascending.

Suddenly understanding, there was hope, the parent felt free to easily take a tiny step in loving the family member, knowing that regardless the parent God would clap. And of course taking one step easily prepares one for taking another. Since then the parent has taken many more steps toward loving more. Self-condemnation, of where we are in life, is worthless.

In addition the parent now metaphorically claps when witnessing any small steps taken by others, not just themselves.

Step by step may all move forward, slow or fast. *"For now You number my steps, You do not observe my sin."* *(Job 14:16)*.

VII) Supportive Format

This abridged commentary rearranges the visions of the Book of Revelation in the same order as in building an archway. To illuminate the parallel structure vision one and seven are presented together, next vision two and six, and then vision three and five. The arch rises and meets in the middle. There, vision four, the keystone, is positioned to declare innocent perfection for all.

Each vision begins with a *preview* and similarly ends with a *summation*. Figures are added to provide clarity of the parallel structure. *Italicized* words, which have no quote nor referenced Bible (book chapter: verse), are taken directly from the Book of Revelation for analytical discussion.

When you see such *italicized* words, find the identical texts in your Bible. Highlight the texts in Revelation with a marker. Then read this book's commentary. Also mark and label your Bible's pages where one vision or section transitions to another. Note: Punctuation marks and the numbering of Bible verses were only recently added by editors in the sixteenth century.

This book's commentary should be simple and practical. Qualities of good over evil are emphasized. Kindness and compassion are promoted. Thus obeying God's will brings more harmony into the world. One selfless act, not seen by man, but seen by God, will do more for the world than one will ever know.

"There was a little city, and few men within it; and there came a great king against it, and besieged it, and built great bulwarks against it: Now there was found in it a poor wise man, and he by his wisdom delivered the city; yet no man remembered that same poor man." (Ecclesiastes 9:14, 15).

Nothing is taken away from studying all the details of Revelation, yet highlighting texts may assist the newcomer in unveiling hard-to-decipher ancient wisdom. It does not need to take a lot of effort to gain unfoldment. Let this new view of the holy visions fortify one across all the seasons of life.

Prior to the seven visions, Revelation begins with two parts: Introduction and Letters.

Introduction

Preview

The Book of Revelation begins with a powerful Introduction. There are seven sections to this Introduction.

I)—Revealing
God   Christ
Holy Spirit Servants

II)—Blessing
Study
Contemplate
Practice

III)—Greeting
Grace & Peace

IV)—Redemption
Corporeal
Moral
Enlightened

V)—Creator
Eternal Almighty

VI)—Creating
Great Voice

VII)—Creation
Divine Expression

"Search the scriptures; for in them ye think ye have eternal life:" (John 5:39). Witness the similar structure of the seven parables from Matthew chapter 13: Spiritual Treasure, Seeking, Sharing, Three Measures, The Planter, The Sprouting, The Net Overflowing.

Introduction

(Rev. 1:1—1:18)

I) Revealing (God, Christ, Spirit, Servants)

(find in your Bible *these words* see Rev. 1:1, 2)
The Revelation ~The Revealing
Christ, God, Servants, Things To Come

Things To Come is liken to the *Holy Ghost*. "*That good thing which was committed unto thee keep by the Holy Ghost which dwelleth in us.*" (II Timothy 1:14). "*ye have an unction from the Holy One, and ye know all things.*" (I John 2:20).

Christ and *God* combined with the *Holy Ghost,* gives rise to the Trinity. Because in monotheism there are no Gods many, this must be a Tri-Unity.

Servants equate to something many do not accept as holy—us! But here it is plain that God's children shall not be left out of Revelation's revealing. "*What is man, that thou art mindful of him?*" (Psalm 8:4). "*he kept him as the apple of his eye.*" (Deuteronomy 32:10). But is this apple of his eye the corporeal Adam? No. Revelation endorses the incorporeal: Prayerful servants in patient service.

Unfortunately modern society endorses selfhood—becoming famous, wealthy, and powerful. Personal centeredness is the modern mantra. Yet everyone is complaining, wanting better "service."

Even the Exemplar's golden rule demands better service. "*whatsoever ye would that men should do to you: do ye even so to them: for this is the law and the prophets.*" (Matthew 7:12). Howbeit if one fails to bless others, life will contain little joy. If one serves, one blesses. "*wrong not, and ye shall not be wronged.*" (2:279). "*thou shalt love thy neighbour as thyself.*" (Leviticus 19:18).

Ask yourself, what good deed did I do today toward someone else? It costs nothing to let someone feel appreciated. Does not being a holy Servant demonstrate on earth the Divine Word, the Christ, and the Holy Spirit? This foursome *Servant(s), God, Christ, Holy Ghost* reveals a superstructure, all good, and without evil.

II) Blessing (Study, Contemplate, Practice)

(find in your Bible *these words* see Rev. 1:3)
readeth ~Study   *hear* ~Contemplate   *keep* ~Practice

Blessed is he that studies, contemplates, and practices Revelation.

Study: Paramount whether in art or science. One cannot excel without it. Study is activity in reasoning, the springboard for any endeavor. *"Study to shew thyself approved unto God, a workman that needeth not to be ashamed, rightly dividing the word of truth." (II Timothy 2:15)*. But study alone falls short of success.

Contemplate: Attune beyond the technical, to where meditative reflection reaches inspiration. Contemplation overcomes the clinical and fulfills heart and soul. The highest form of listening is communing with the mental hieroglyphs from the nature of the universe. *"in his law doth he meditate day and night." (Psalm 1:2)*.

Practice: Study and Contemplation escorts us into Practice. Here reason and inspiration are demonstrated. Mentors constantly advise practice. Practice, and more practice is required to improve. Be humble in the doing and in being corrected. Practice is not talking and telling, it is reason and inspiration demonstrated. *"Those things, which ye have both learned, and received, and heard, and seen in me, do:" (Philippians 4:9)*.

Think this is all too hard? Well then if one is not striving to be a better asset to the world, then one is by default dragging it down. What one tends to do is what one is. But anyone can reverse any stumbling. *"submit yourselves therefore to God. Resist the devil, and he will flee from you" (James 4:7)*.

Study, Contemplate, and Practice. Apply reason, inspiration, and demonstration. These three will let us rise above the mist and debris, allowing us to be of better service to the world. Blessing others, blesses us.

III) Greeting (Shalom Aleichem; Salaam Alaykum)

(find in your Bible *these words* see Rev. 1:4, 5, 6)
grace [be] unto you, and peace ~Greetings of Grace/Peace

Prayerful servants in patient service greet each other with reverence.

A hospitable greeting in Hebrew is Sholem Aleichem; in Arabic it is As-Salamu Alaikum (or similar spellings for both). Let us greet everyone with love everyday in life when meeting and parting.

Greet everyone and anyone as a member of the holy family chosen by God. In the Tanakh, *"He who is gracious to a poor man lends to the Lord, and He will repay him his reward." (Proverbs 19:17)*. In the New Testament, *"And now, brethren, I commend you to God, and to the word of his grace, which is able to build you up, and to give you an inheritance among all them which are sanctified." (Acts 20:32)*. In the Quran, *"treat with kindness your parents and kindred, and orphans and those in need; speak fair to the people;" (2:83)*.

Note that a greeting of grace and peace are at-one with God, Holy Spirit, Christ, and Servants, i.e., *Him, seven Spirits, Christ, Us kings and priests*.

Holy greetings to others is our inherent purpose. No one is beneath anyone else. All are honored beings when grace is observed.

IV) Redemption (Corporeal, Moral, Enlightened)

(find in your Bible *these words* see Rev. 1:7)
every eye shall see him ~Corporeal state
they also which pierced him ~Moral state
all kindreds of the earth ~Enlightened state

Many ancient philosophies and religions identify differing levels, or states of consciousness. Typically there is an unenlightened base, then some transitional states, and finally an enlightened state. Esoteric treatises describe the human and the God-conscious states (Taqwaa in Arabic; Tzelem in Hebrew).

The Corporeal state: Believes only the evidence of the five senses—what the *eye* can see. This state contains pleasure, pain, fear, vengeance, etc. Yet science proves corporeal sense is deceptive; such as in optical illusions, hypnotism, and the placebo effect—a beneficiary effect that cannot be attributed to physics and must therefore be due to perception (including the nocebo effect). *"the eye is not satisfied with seeing," (Ecclesiastes 1:8).*

The Moral state: Faith in overcoming immorality. Morality tirelessly struggles to subdue the pleasures and pains of corporeality. Often a quandary appears, on what action to take. The moralist answers the question—if everyone did it, and did it most of the time, would the world be in a better state? To *pierce* anyone with words or deeds unkind does the world no good.

The Enlightened state: Understanding sweeps away storms. Holy love is cloudless. *"I have swept away your offenses like a cloud, your sins like the morning mist. Return to me, for I have redeemed you" (Isaiah 44:22).* *"children of the prophets, ... kindreds of the earth." (Acts 3:25).*

Trials *wail* metaphorically, like clouds obscuring light. Yet dark trials teach grand lessons, *"seek good, and not evil, that ye may live:" (Amos 5:14).* The enlightened state acts upon the moral state to overcome the trials of the corporeal state. The higher state should always help the lower. *"Bear ye one another's burdens, and so fulfil the law of Christ." (Galatians 6:2).*

V) Creator (Eternal, Almighty)

(find in your Bible *these words* see Rev. 1:8)
I Am ~Creator
the beginning and the ending
Almighty

"*I AM THAT I AM:*" *(Exodus 3:14).* *I Am* can be nothing less than the Creator. The Eternal is now, *the beginning and the ending*. And the appearance is *Almighty*. "*And Jacob said unto Joseph, God Almighty appeared unto me*" *(Genesis 48:3).* Corporeality, even morality, has no part with the self-abnegating enlightened. "*I can of mine own self do nothing:*" *(John 5:30).*

Let us examine the first words of the Holy Bible. Consider that one is at the edge of history, listening to a great holy being. Firstly, primordial sounds are heard. Proto-Sinaitic scribes mark the first three beginning root words of the Bible: Bara Bara Elohim (from right to left, Creator Creating Creation). Note: it does not infer the Creator and Creation ever had a beginning.

Secondly, the holy being points to a sky above. One scribe writes, heaven. Another, the infinite. The holy one then picks up a spec of earth. One scribe writes, earth. Another, the infinitesimal.

Many consider that the earth was "without form, & void." The Hebrew words are tohu and bohu (formless and mindless). The counter-fact, or antipode, would be *substance* and *intelligence*.

Consider the opening phrases of Genesis as:

"Creator Creates Creation
from the Infinite to the Infinitesimal.
Even the smallest infinitesimal principle
Is not unlike substance & intelligence
For ignorance lies in the abyss.
And the inspiration of Elohim
Nurtures the waters (ideas of Spirit)."

This nurturing leads to the next verses in the Bible revealing the *I Am* in seven parts—the Seven Days of the Creator Creating Creation (Genesis chapter one).

VI) Creating (Great Voice)

(find in your Bible *these words* see Rev. 1:9–11)
great voice ~Creating, Unfolding

The Word speaks; thus ideas come into formation. The creating activity of the divine is likened to a resounding call to prayer, from the high tower or consciousness of the Divine. The uplifting messages of the Christ and Holy Spirit reach out in all directions. It is so written, that the royal creative declarations permeate all with seven-fold completeness and perfection. *"Hear attentively the noise of his voice, and the sound that goeth out of his mouth." (Job 37:2)*. Study, contemplate, and practice creativity and see how that improves everyday life. Express creativity. Journaling about the wonderment of blessings refreshes each day.

"Out of heaven he made thee to hear his voice, that he might instruct thee:" (Deuteronomy 4:36). The creative process is not turbulent as in natural disasters. God loves the earth. *"the earth is full of the goodness of the Lord." (Psalm 33:5)*. The creative process is great yet gentle. *"behold, the Lord passed by, and a great and strong wind rent the mountains, and brake in pieces the rocks before the Lord; but the Lord was not in the wind: and after the wind an earthquake; but the Lord was not in the earthquake: And after the earthquake a fire; but the Lord was not in the fire: and after the fire a still small voice." (I Kings 19:11, 12)*.

This great yet gentle voice cannot be silenced by evil. The Divine is always heard calling to those that struggle and seek, for Job heard it as a lion roareth. *"God thundereth marvellously with his voice; great things doeth he," (Job 37:5)*.

Let us express God with creative activity for good.

VII) Creation (Divine Expression)

(find in your Bible *these words* see Rev. 1:12–18)
like unto the Son of man ~Divine Expression

God's creation is full of divine ideas or expressions. Their generic totality is represented here with bodily symbols. These symbols are not material but are symbolic to be further translated to the mental realm. The head, eyes, feet, voice, hand, mouth, and face are metaphysical elements of distinctiveness. These functional objects represent properties that express a complete manifestation of Creation:

head	All wise
eyes	All seeing
feet	All understanding
voice	All praising
hand	All powerful
mouth	All just/merciful
countenance	All illuminating

"For ye are all the children of God by faith in Christ Jesus." *(Galatians 3:26)*. Thus living more morally and more metaphysically, expression expands into a more complete and harmonious form.

Fear not is a keynote of God Creating Creation. Study, contemplate, and practice the all wise, all seeing, all understanding, all praising, all powerful, all just/merciful, all illuminating to stamp out fear, ignorance, and ill health.

Fear is where one decides to not trust in expressing good deeds, fearing such expressions will be taken advantage of. Then self-will becomes the expression of a less-than-perfect day, forgetting our spiritual being. *"Fear not, little flock; for it is your Father's good pleasure to give you the kingdom."* *(Luke 12:32)*.

Let us express the seven all-inclusive holy qualities in form and deed. These are the keys to overcoming moments of hell in everyday life, thus experiencing more heavenly harmony.

Introduction

Summation

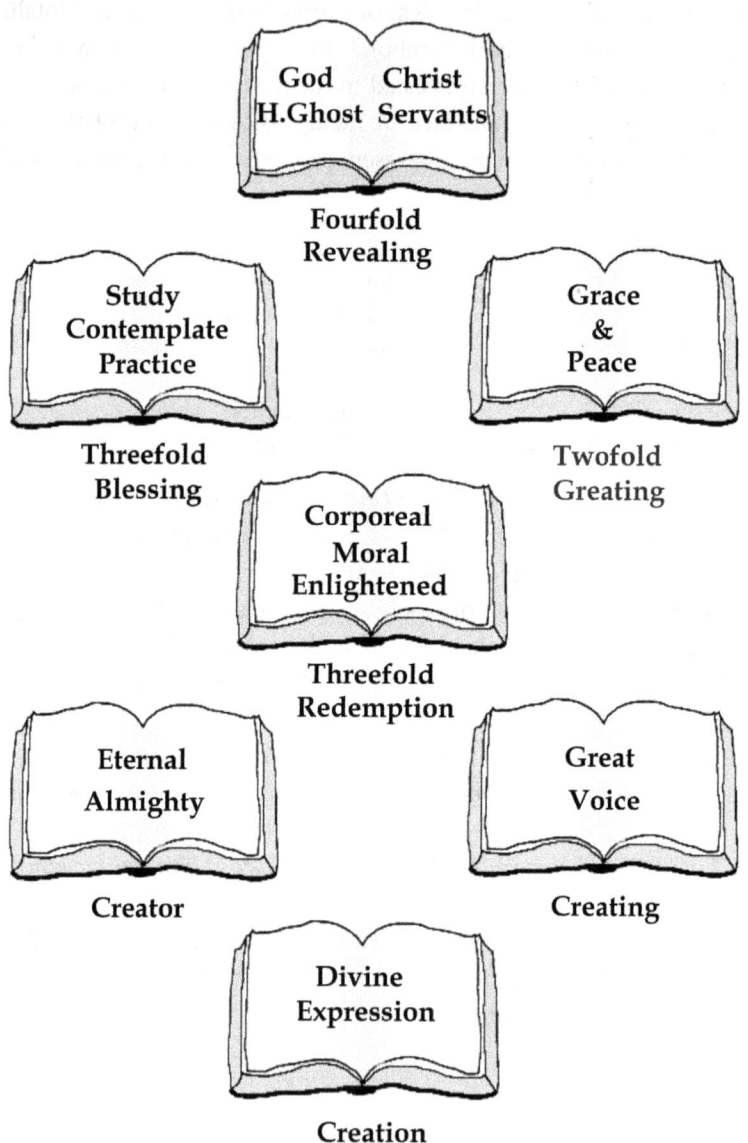

Letters

Preview

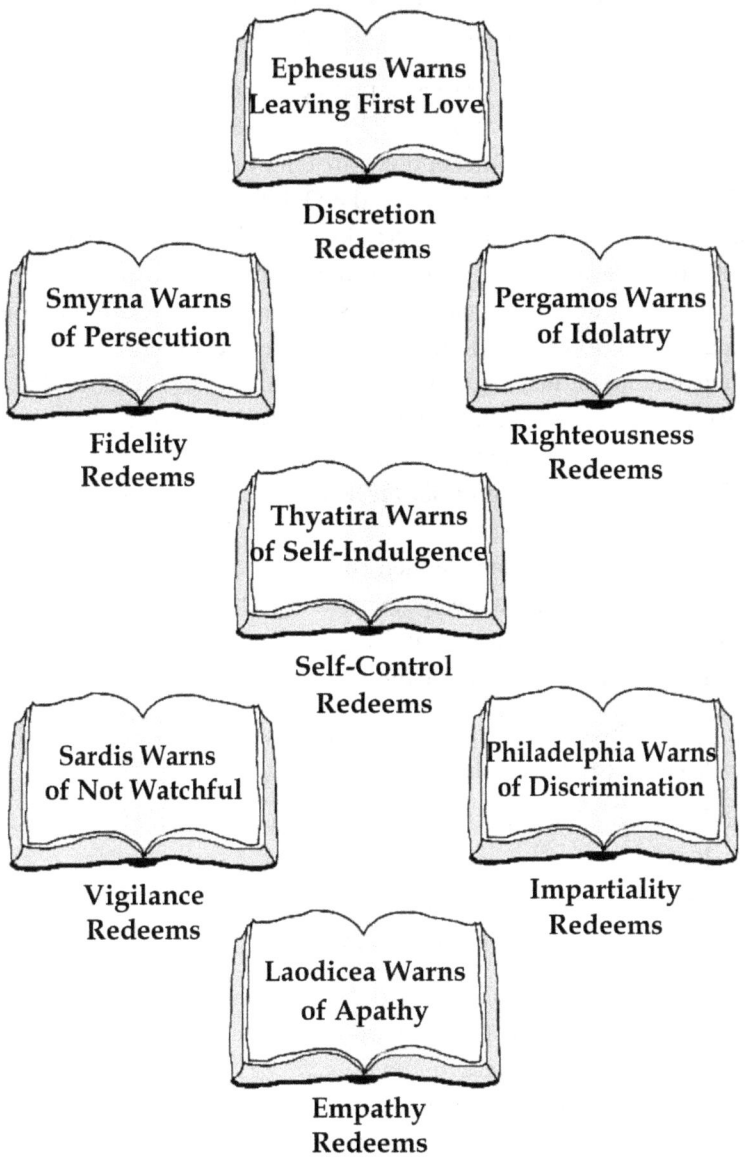

Letters

(Rev. 1:19—3:22)

(find in your Bible *these words* see Rev. 1:19)
Write, the seven churches ~Messages

The seven churches can serve as a prophesy. For example Ephesus is described as the apostolic church (A.D. 30–100), Smyrna as the persecuted (A.D. 100–313), etc. Another option is that these messages taken in sequential follows the Biblical timeline of the Old Testament. Thereby Ephesus corresponds to the antediluvian creation period, Smyrna to the patriarch period of Joseph & Moses, Pergamos to the time of Elijah & Elisha, etc.

Consider too, the seven messages or letters to be addressed to individual consciousness. Then these messages are not concerned with history telling, but are for meeting individual unfoldment. Yes, *Write* to *the seven churches*—where we are the churches. *"Know ye not that ye are the temple of God, and that the Spirit of God dwelleth in you? If any man defile the temple of God, him shall God destroy; for the temple of God is holy, which temple ye are" (I Corinthians 3:16–17).*

If the body is the temple then consider these seven messages as the chakras of individualized metaphysical being. The chakras are mental, not physical. The mystery is church universal.

Each of these seven-in-one messages contain three components:

1. Identifying the cancerous idiosyncrasies in thought and deed that keeps us from harmony,
2. Identifying the graceful qualities in thought and deed that brings us to harmony,
3. Identifying the obedient selflessness in thought and deed that crowns us with a blessing benediction.

These components also parallel the three states of consciousness spoken of in the section titled Introduction: from the Corporeal, to the Moral, and to the Enlightened state.

The following pages provide a quick overview of the letters to the seven churches; seven modes of thought.

I) Ephesus (Discretion—antediluvian Creation Stories)

(find in your Bible *these words* see Rev. 2:1–7)
Left thy first love ~False   *tree of life* ~Benediction

The antediluvian period is the time before the great flood. This is the time of the three creation stories. Beginning the Bible is the Seven Days of Creation story, then the Adam and Eve story, and ending is the Noah and Ark creation story.

Firstly, according to this Ephesus message, what cancerous idiosyncrasy keeps us from harmony? *Left thy first love* indicates not following the enlightened values voiced in the Seven Days of Creation where all is "good." *Remember therefore from whence thou art fallen* indicates having fallen into the mist and dust of the Adam & Eve creation story, whereby believing in the coexistence of good and evil. Without discretion, knowing good from evil, one forgets the good and follows the evil, like Adam.

Secondly, what graceful quality in thought and deed brings us to harmony? *Do the first works*. What are the first works? It is the Seven Days unfolding spiritual understanding. Spiritual discernment removes the temptation to live like Adam & Eve (believing in the corporeal senses to know both good and evil); or to live like Noah and his family (struggling to remain morally faithful). Unfortunately a constant theme runs throughout the Bible: the people follow God for a while, then turn away, and then through suffering return once again to God. *"choose you this day whom ye will serve; whether the gods which your fathers served that were on the other side of the flood, or the gods of the Amorites," (Joshua 24:15)*.

Thirdly, what selfless obedience crowns us with a blessing benediction for replacing ignorance, fear, and depravity with discernment? The freedom to eat from the *tree of life*.

In summary the Ephesus message is to maintain spiritual discretion. Discernment is the counter-fact to ignorance. In the Quran, *"He lays abomination upon those who do not reason or understand" (10:100)*. In the Tanakh, *"They also that err in spirit shall come to understanding" (Isaiah 29:24)*. For more harmony in daily life, discern between good and evil, and hold on to the good.

II) Smyrna (Fidelity—patriarchs Joseph/Moses)

(find in your Bible *these words* see Rev. 2:8–11)
tribulation ten days ~False   *shall not be hurt* ~Benediction

The patriarchal period began with Abraham and Sarah, and may have ended with or before the Exodus from Egypt. In any event *cast [some] of you into prison* is reminiscent of Joseph being sold and taken to Egypt. This eventually lead to the twelve tribes becoming slaves of the pharaohs. The *tribulation ten days* is reminiscent of the ten plagues of Moses, which led to the Exodus. Certainly during all this time in Egypt the captive children of God were persecuted and blasphemed.

Firstly, according to this Smyrna message, what cancerous idiosyncrasy keeps us from harmony? Without fidelity there is *blasphemy* and persecution. Did not the myrrh presented at the savior's birth and death suggest that the holy are persecuted by those that blaspheme?

Secondly, what graceful quality in thought and deed brings us to harmony? *Faithful unto death.* Faithfulness can be defined as reverence, requiring great fidelity. Fidelity is consecrated patience during oppressive persecution.

Thirdly, what selfless obedience crowns us with a blessing benediction for replacing ignorance, fear, and depravity with fidelity? Ye *shall not be hurt of the second death.*

In summary the Smyrna message is to maintain fidelity. Persecution is overcome by the trustworthy. Trustworthiness is the counter-fact to faithlessness. In the Quran, *"in Allah should the faithful put their trust"* (9:51). In the Tanakh, *"put your trust in the Lord"* (Psalm 3:1).

For more harmony in daily life, hold on to fidelity.

III) Pergamos (Righteousness—prophets Elijah & Elisha)

(find in your Bible *these words* see Rev. 2:12–17)
stumbling block ~False   *white stone* ~Benediction

The period of prophets, including Elijah and Elisha, had to deal with stumbling blocks of ungodliness. Balaam and other idolatry caused the tribes to stumble repeatedly. Howbeit the prophets continually urged the people to strike down idolatry and fornication, clear away black stones of guilt, and be righteous.

Firstly, according to this Pergamos message, what cancerous idiosyncrasy keeps us from harmony? Impurity, *doctrine of Balaam*. Idolatry, wickedness, and unrighteousness are a *stumbling block*.

Secondly, what graceful quality in thought and deed brings us to harmony? Righteousness. Righteousness refuses both *to eat things sacrificed unto idols, and to commit fornication*.

Thirdly, what selfless obedience crowns us with a blessing benediction for replacing ignorance, fear, and depravity with righteousness? A *white stone*. Traditionally small stones were used in voting; white for innocent, black for guilty.

In summary the Pergamos message is to maintain righteousness. Righteous service can be defined as unadulterated & uncontaminated. Righteousness is the counter-fact to wickedness. In the Quran, *"Zakariya and John, and Jesus and Elias: all in the ranks of the righteous:"* (6:85). In the Tanakh, *"And you shall return and discern between the righteous and the wicked, between him who serves God and him who has not served Him"* (Malachi 3:18).

For more harmony in daily life, hold on to righteousness.

IV) Thyatira (Self-Control—kings Saul & David)

(find in your Bible *these words* see Rev. 2:18–28)
prophetess ~False   *power over the nations* ~Benediction

During this timeframe Saul strayed away from following God, for when fearing ruin he called for a *prophetess* to gain victory over his enemies. Self-will was his downfall. The following king, David, also strayed and *committed adultery* with Beersheba. Later he murdered her husband, Uriah the Hittite.

Firstly, according to this Thyatira message, what cancerous idiosyncrasy keeps us from harmony? Self-indulgence, lack of self-control. Selfish life motives lead to self-ruin. Here there is no service to mankind.

Secondly, what graceful quality in thought and deed brings us to harmony? Self-control. By governing ourselves, one is able to witness our holy service to yourself, to families, as well as to nations.

Thirdly, what selfless obedience crowns us with a blessing benediction for replacing ignorance, fear, and depravity with self-control? *Power over the nations*. Self-control rewards with power over mind and body, thus being an example for others to follow. Likewise, King David repented, grew in self-control, and became and example for others to follow.

In summary the Thyatira message is to maintain self-control. Self-restraint is the counter-fact to self-will. In the Quran, *"O David! . . . do not follow the whims of your own soul for they will lead you astray from God's path"* (38:26). In the Tanakh, *"Like a city broken down and without a wall, So is he whose spirit is without restraint"* (Proverbs 25:28).

For more harmony in daily life, hold on to self-control.

V) Sardis (Vigilance—schism Israel/Judah)

(find in your Bible *these words* see Rev. 3:1–6)
shalt not watch ~False   *not blot out his name* ~Benediction

Historically after the period of Kings the Hebrew nation split apart, a schism between north and south. Like so many other times in history across the world, schisms arise over who is to become the next leader. Unfortunately when nations become divided, foreigners easily invade and conquer. With the descendants of Isaac, this resulted in a diaspora of the Jews. With the descendants of Ishmael (Isaac's brother), this resulted in a schism—between Islamic Shiites and Sunnis (over who was to be the next leader).

Firstly, according to this Sardis message, what cancerous idiosyncrasy keeps us from harmony? Slothfulness that *shalt not watch*. Not guarding against the enemy within—which always results in schisms—allows the external enemy to enter and break up what good thou hast within. Not being watchful allows the dividing asunder, brother against brother. No person should ever divide a family, company, or nation into warring factions.

Secondly, what graceful quality in thought and deed brings us to harmony? *Be watchful.* Be vigilant against the foes by obeying one God leader, and loving thy neighbor. *"Watch therefore: for ye know not what hour your Lord doth come. But know this, that if the goodman of the house had known in what watch the thief would come, he would have watched, and would not have suffered his house to be broken up."* (Matthew 24:42, 43).

Thirdly, what selfless obedience crowns us with a blessing benediction for replacing ignorance, fear, and depravity with vigilance? *I will not blot out his name.* Vigilance will find common ground to prevent any tear in the fabric of alliances.

In summary the Sardis message is watchfulness. Vigilance is the counter-fact to slothfulness in not watching. In the Quran *"a favor from your Lord. that is the supreme salvation . . . so wait and watch"* (44:57–59). In the Tanakh, *"For thus hath the Lord said unto me: Go, set a watchman; Let him declare what he seeth!"* (Isaiah 21:6).

For more harmony in daily life, hold on to vigilance.

VI) Philadelphia (Impartiality—returning Remnant)

(find in your Bible *these words* see Rev. 3:7–13)
but do lie ~False   *pillar in the temple* ~Benediction

After the dispersion of the Hebrew tribes, Esther became queen and her marriage gave the Hebrews prestige in the Persian court. This lessening of hatred between nations later allowed Ezra and Nehemiah to begin rebuilding the temple walls with the remnant peoples of God. In like manner, building or rebuilding relationships is not easy, but impartiality quickens the labor.

Firstly, according to this Philadelphia message, what cancerous idiosyncrasy keeps us from restoring harmony? Selective discrimination, those that say they follow the teachings of God, *but do lie*, because they love not all their neighbors. Expressing impartiality can build or rebuild lives, families, communities, and nations that are lasting and without partiality. Discrimination shuts the door on building soundly.

Secondly, what graceful quality in thought and deed brings us to harmony? Un-discriminatory love. Unequivocal love for everyone is *an open door* allowing all to enter and to be greeted with equanimity.

Thirdly, what selfless obedience crowns us with a blessing benediction for replacing ignorance, fear, and depravity with impartiality? The inalienable right to become a *pillar in the temple*. Pillars are those, who not by appointment, but by heartfelt love, stand as church mentors. Their upright deeds of loving impartially (like the five inspirational pillars of Islam) support those at home, at work, and in the community.

In summary the Philadelphia message is to build without partiality. Build sound relationships internally and externally. Impartiality is the counter-fact to partiality and discrimination. In the Quran, *"Allah loves the doers of good." (2:195)*. In the Tanakh, *"The stranger that sojourneth with you shall be unto you as the home-born among you," (Leviticus 19:34)*.

For more harmony in daily life, hold on to universal love. Have compassion—especially for those with opposing sentiments.

VII) Laodicea (Empathy—occupation by Rome)

(find in your Bible *these words* see Rev. 3:14–22)
neither cold nor hot ~False   *sit with me* ~Benediction

During the Roman occupation of the Near East, many inhumane acts where witnessed. It took around a hundred years before the Hebrews united in revolt. Look across the world at where thought still succumbs to physical and mental tyranny.

Firstly, according to this Laodicea message, what cancerous idiosyncrasy keeps us from harmony? Apathy as to what is happening. *Thou art neither cold nor hot*. Indifference allows all sorts of unethical extortion, corruption, trafficking, etc. to creep in and pollute nature, mind, and body.

Secondly, what graceful quality in thought and deed brings us to harmony? Empathy. Let there be empathy: to help those going through fiery trials, *tried in the fire*; to help those that are unprotected, *nakedness*; and to help those who are blind to the foe in ambush, *anoint thine eyes*.

Thirdly, what selfless obedience crowns us with a blessing benediction for replacing ignorance, fear, and depravity with empathy? To *sit with me* (Lord). Empathy and standing up for others provides audience with the Holy. Empathy is the counter-fact to apathy.

In summary the Laodicea message is to maintain empathy and compassion for neighbors. In the Quran, *"advised one another to patience and advised one another to compassion." (90:17)*. In the Tanakh, *"Thus hath the Lord of hosts spoken, saying: Execute true judgment, and show mercy and compassion every man to his brother;" (Zechariah 7:9)*.

For more harmony in daily life, hold on to empathy.

Letters
Summation

The letters to the churches unfold the spiritual awakenings of the Old Testament in seven stages. These awakenings allowed the coming of the Messiah. Therefore, express more of these seven qualities for more harmony in life.

I)—Discretion
Reflective of the antediluvian creation stories
Ephesus warns of: leaving first love for an unholy creation

II)—Fidelity
Reflective of the patriarchs Joseph & Moses
Smyrna warns of: blasphemy & persecution

III)—Righteousness
Reflective of the prophets Elijah & Elisha
Pergamos warns of: idolatry & fornication

IV)—Self-Control
Reflective of the kings Saul & David
Thyatira warns of: self-indulgence

V)—Vigilance
Reflective of the Israel/Judah schism
Sardis warns of: being not watchful

VI)—Impartiality
Reflective of the rebuilding remnant
Philadelphia warns of: discriminatory love

VII)—Empathy
Reflective of the Roman occupation
Laodicea warns of: apathy

After the Introduction and Letters of Revelation, the Seven Visions appear. Pairing of these visions; comparing vision one to seven, vision two to six, and vision three to five, produces unique clarity to the structure of Revelation: Plus the forth vision is the keystone, the centerpiece, the statement of being, declaring that all spiritual ideas manifest only innocent perfection.

If you agree that spiritual identity is innocent perfection, then perhaps your own spiritual identity can play a bigger part in this world. Across history there have been many great thinkers that have promoted a vision of peace, equality, and kindness. What would the world be like if those individuals had instead promoted stealing, lying, and greed? Clearly any individual that expresses a little more grace each day, improves the world; while becoming a better example for humanity. Therefore, deeds of kindness, which exemplifies a better understanding of spiritual identity, can brighten our own surroundings—thus the world.

The visions of the apocalypse display much woes and violence, but these are just counter-facts of innocent perfection. By understanding Revelation one finds that the destructive elements of mortality are always overturned to forward the Creator's design. Motives and deeds that depart from the Divine Goodness will keep varying their malicious ways, yet never prospering. Carnal confidence, trying to surface throughout Revelation, is defeated by the structural integrity of supreme wisdom. *"For we wrestle not against flesh and blood, but against principalities." (Ephesians 6:12).*

Vision One

Preview

*The Lord is my shepherd,
I shall not want.*

(PSALM 23)

In vision one of Revelation the "great shepherds" of the Old Testament & New Testament complement. Seven symbols of Moses' Tabernacle from Exodus are embodied, then re-envisioned in the Lord's Prayer from Matthew. Moses' moral unfoldment of worship and justice is supported and elevated by Jesus Christ's enlightened unfoldment of worship and mercy.

	Moses Tabernacle	Lord's Prayer
I)	Holy of Holies	Our Father
II)	Cherubim	Which art in Heaven
III)	Incense	Hollowed Thy Name
IVa)	Lamp's Light	Thy Kingdom Come
		Thy will be done
IVb)	Four Ensigns	In Earth as in Heaven
V)	Table of Showbread	Give us Daily Bread
VI)	Laver of Water	Pure Forgiving
VII)	Altar of Sacrifice	Lead not into Temptation

Vision Seven

Preview

*I will dwell in the house
of the Lord forever*
(PSALM 23)

In vision seven of Revelation the "great scribes" of the Old Testament & New Testament complement. Seven symbols of the Seven Days of Creation from Genesis are embodied, then re-envisioned in the Holy City from the Revelation of John. Creation is unfolded having ample justice and mercy. Creation from Genesis is cognizant of the bride, the Holy Spirit

	Holy City	Seven Days
I)	City of Cities	Light, Energy
II)	Precious Clarity	Heaven, Discernment
III)	Praise & Salvation	Growth & Identity
IVa)	Glory's Light	Universe Coincident
IVb)	Four-Square	Universal Order
V)	Book of Life	Angelic Sustenance
VI)	Water of Life	Pure Offspring
VII)	Tree of Life	Sanctification

*Vision One
Holy Tabernacle (Rev. 4:1—5:14)

*The Lord is my shepherd;
I shall not want.*

(PSALM 23:1)

(find in your Bible *these words* see Rev. 4:1,2)
[one] sat on the throne ~Fatherhood

Fatherhood expresses Monotheism, given by the great shepherds like Abraham with his alter to the one God. Later the shepherd Moses saw *a door [was] opened in heaven*. Elohim spoke and Moses set up a portable altar or Tabernacle. Now for the people of God, began a journey of learning on how to spiritualize the worshiping of the Divine.

[One] sat on the throne, and patriarchs communed mentally with Elohim. Yet the people still hungered after physical means and methods to worship, and in following centuries other material edifices were constructed with more diverse rituals and oftentimes dogmas.

Thankfully transcendental seekers strove to look beyond the veil and reach beyond the corporeal. In the Quran, *"My Lord, build for me, with you, a house in Paradise" (66:11)*. In the Tanakh, *"For I desire mercy, and not sacrifice, and the knowledge of God rather than burnt-offerings." (Hosea 6:6)*.

There are seven major Tabernacle items used by Moses (Exodus 25). Let us take these physical objects of worship and exchanged them for mental symbols. Thus, another link appears. Brilliantly, the major seven object-symbols of the Old Testament's Tabernacle of Moses align with the major seven parts of the New Testament's Lord's Prayer (Matthew 5).

The Shepherd, Jesus Christ, understood Moses' metaphysical concept of worship. When Jesus was asked by followers how to worship—or pray, he translated thought from physical rituals to metaphysical practices. This comparison of the Old and New Testament worship agrees with Jesus Christ's statement, *"I am not come to destroy, but to fulfill." (Matthew 5:17)*. See what Jesus said to the Samaritan woman at the well regarding where one worships (John 4:4-24). The Fatherhood's desire is to spiritualize worship.

The following pages provide a quick overview of vision one.

*Vision Seven

Holy City (Rev. 21:9—22:2)

*and I will dwell
in the house of the Lord for ever.*
(PSALM 23)

(find in your Bible *these words* see Rev. 21:9)
the bride ~Motherhood

Motherhood, expressed by the Holy Spirit, comforts. She appears as *the bride*. The Tanakh says, *"Like someone comforted by his mother, I will comfort you; in Yerushalayim you will be comforted."* (Isaiah 66:13). The Quran says, *"No doubt, in the remembrance of Allah hearts find comfort."* (13:28).

Earlier, vision one focused on the Holy Tabernacle and *groom*. Now in vision seven comes the Holy City and *bride*. These two visions form a marriage between the Old and New Testaments. Also, where vision one had the Tabernacle corresponding to the Lord's Prayer, inversely vision seven has the major symbolic parts of the New Testament city in Revelation corresponding to the Old Testament creation stories in Genesis.

Note there are three creation stories in the beginning of Genesis, each written by factions with differing ideas about the nature of God. 1) The Seven Day Creation story is based on an Elohistic document where God is called Elohim in Hebrew. 2) The Adam & Eve story is based on a Jehovistic document where God is called Jehovah in Hebrew. 3) The Noah & Ark story is based on a Priestly document where God is called Yahweh in Hebrew.

In comparing these creation stories with the symbolism of the Holy City, it becomes reasonably evident that the Motherhood of God is purest in The Seven Day Creation story. In each day Elohim saw everything that he made . . . and behold it was "very good."

The *second death* does not affect he that overcometh. The total self-annihilation of evil never touches he that is the servant of the Elohim. Notice that in these city-creation discussions that follow, Motherhood's desire is to comfort.

The following pages provide a quick overview of vision seven.

I) Holy of Holies (Our Father)
Vision One

(find in your Bible *these words* see Rev. 4:1–2)
a throne was set in heaven ~Immortal Structure

The Holy of Holies is an inner sanctuary within the Tabernacle outlined by Moses. This is likened to a throne room, for here resided the Arc of the Covenant. "... *to us there is but one God, the Father, of whom are all things,*" *(I Corinthians 8:6).*

Under the Mosaic law only the male high priest could perform the atonement. But what says the New Testament—all are high priests and priestess unto God (see Revelation 1:6). Thus can anyone be deprived of meditating directly with the Divine Father?

Any prayerful servant in patient service has the right to the atonement with the Father, at any time and at any place, male or female. So be it, in the Lord's Prayer, *"Our Father,"* where God is ever at hand. "*Thou art my father, my God, and the rock of my salvation.*" *(Psalm 89:26).* Our rock or throne of salvation resides within the inner sanctuary—in consciousness.

The seat of consciousness, where *a throne was set in heaven,* is a mental sacred place. In this meditative state one can embrace the metaphysical four planes of the Holy of Holies: "*The grace of the Lord Jesus 'Christ,' and the love of 'God', and the fellowship of the 'Holy Spirit,' be with 'you all'* (servants)." *(II Corinthians 13:14).*

Vision one parallels the seventh vision, i.e., the Tabernacle for the *groom* is likened to the City for the *bride*. And so let us receive a benediction as priests and priestesses to worship rightly the Father/Mother Divine.

Be a disciple of Christ by sharing more of God's goodness and grace.

I) City of Cities (Light)
Vision Seven

(find in your Bible *these words* see Rev. 21:9–10)
that great city ~Immoral Structure

From the great and high mountain is seen the revealing light shining resplendent, *that great city*. "*O send out thy light and thy truth: let them lead me; let them bring me unto thy holy hill*" *(Psalm 43:3)*. This city, a spiritual utopia, is the opposite of a distopia.

Day one of seven from Genesis Elohim said, *"let there be light . . . and it was good." (Genesis 1:3, 4).*

Light is considered radiant energy. Yet, this is only a hint of the ever-operating metaphysical symbolism. Energy is not from the "big bang theory" but is the Creator Creating Creation. Nature hints at the true essence. Enlightened being reveals, brightens, guides, and so much more.

Light is omnipresent love as shown with Jesus Christ's healing of two blind men (see Matthew 9:27–29). Darkness and suffering is not God's will. Such ignorance the Son healed. So be not ignorant. "*Woe unto you, . . . hypocrites! . . . and have omitted the weightier matters of the law, judgment, mercy, and faith: these ought ye to have done, and not to leave the other undone. Ye blind guides, which strain at a gnat, and swallow a camel.*" *(Matthew 23:23, 24).*

* Regarding the creation stories of Genesis: Day one of seven corresponds to the Adam & Eve story and the mist (Genesis 2:6). Mist obscures. It blurs. It prevents focusing on the good only. Day one also corresponds to the Noah & Ark story and grace (Genesis 6:8, 9). Morality keeps the light of wisdom with self-abnegating grace and is rewarded by God's favor.

Be a follower of the Holy Spirit by sharing more of God's comforting power and patience.

II) Cherubim (in Heaven)
Vision One

(find in your Bible *these words* see Rev. 4:3)
like a jasper and a sardine stone ~Cherubim

The two Cherubim rise over the throne or Arc of the Covenant. These foundational symbols radiate, *like a jasper and a sardine stone*, and exemplify the grandeur of heaven. *"Let us draw near with confidence to the throne of grace, so that we may receive mercy and find grace to help in time of need." (Hebrew 4:16).*

Jasper and sardine, are likened to the beginning and ending of the twelve stones in the breastplate of the priest (Exodus 28:17–21). Like a rainbow these radiant colorful gems were worn during the ceremony of atonement.

Likewise in the Lord's Prayer the rainbow of heaven is a prism of hues radiating goodness. Jesus Christ reveals an elevated mindset of the two inner sanctuary Cherubim when he said in the Lord's Prayer, *"which art in Heaven."*

Heaven contains two great commands, exemplified by the two Cherubim of principle, justice and mercy. *"Justice and judgment are the habitation of thy throne: mercy and truth shall go before thy face." (Psalm 89:14).* The two are also likened to a two-edged sword.

The two great commands summarize Moses' ten, i.e., five teach to love God, and the other five teach to love thy neighbor. This heavenly pair also teach the difference between right and wrong, the firmament separating corporeal illusion from enlightened reality.

Let us receive a benediction as priests and priestesses to worship (embrace) in spirit the reflective symbols of holy justice and mercy. With these, great discernment is possible, seeing past any veil and bringing more harmony into every day experience.

II) Precious Clarity (Heaven)
Vision Seven

(find in your Bible *these words* see Rev. 21:10, 11)
a stone most precious ~Precious Clarity

Heaven is spoken of many times in the New Testament with, "heaven is liken to . . ." Thus considering heaven as a state of mind. *"the kingdom of God is at hand:" (Mark 1:15). A stone most precious, Clear as crystal,* is clarity and insight, straight *out of heaven.*

Day two of seven from Genesis Elohim said, *"Let there be a firmament." (Genesis 1:6).* The firmament discerns between ideas (water), between the true and the false; *"divided the waters which were under the firmament from the waters which were above the firmament:" (Genesis 1:7).* Insight washes away evil from good, thus bringing clarity.

Insight is shown by Jesus Christ's healing of the lunatic, removing insanity from sanity (see Matthew 17: 14-18). This vision of Revelation shows a precious city within heaven. It is the opposite of the egotistic tower of Babel. *"let us build us a city and a tower, whose top may reach unto heaven; and let us make us a name," (Genesis 11:4).* Insight is the yea, yea; nay, nay of the Bible.

Heaven clear as crystal is reflective clarity. Heaven allows infinite variety. The source is one, yet the rays many. One is cause. The other is effect.

* Regarding the creation stories of Genesis: Day two of seven corresponds to the Adam & Eve story and the dust (Genesis 2:7). Dust confuses thinking. Dust adulterates the clear and reflective. Together dust and mist create mud. Without clarity there is no spotless form. Day two also corresponds to the Noah & Ark story and the flood (Genesis 6:17); morality washing away the evil dust. The flood is a moral regenerative response to corporeality.

Comfort others by sharing more clarity and focusing on the shining goodness.

III) Altar of Incense (Hallowed Name)
Vision One

(find in your Bible *these words* see Rev. 4:4, 5)
lightnings and thunderings . . . voices ~Altar of Incense

Incense, like *voices*, praise and rise to heaven (see Revelation 5:8: elders with golden vials of odours). *"Let my prayer be set forth before thee [as] incense;" (Psalm 141:2).* In many cultures incense is a symbol of a resilient appeal, like ardent *lightnings and thunderings*.

Islamic pilgrims of the Kaaba have fifty hallowed names for Allah; Jewish followers of the Kabbala have fifty gates of hallowed understanding. Search Revelation and discover the many names and attributes that belong to the hallowed Elohim.

In the Lord's Prayer, Jesus Christ reveals an elevated mindset of the altar of incense when he said in the Lord's Prayer, *"Hallowed by Thy Name."*

The *four and twenty elders* are wise and learned. They represent life full of praise, life consecrated. *"Neither shall ye profane my holy name; but I will be hallowed . . ." (Leviticus 22:32).*

Similarly, the Sermon on the Mount has twenty-four sequential sections (Matthew chapters 5–7). These too hold great wisdom. Suggested subtitles (or create your own study outline).

Sermon on the Mount twenty-four sections

1. God's Blessings	2. Light & Salt
3. Principle	4. Anger vs Reconcile
5. Lust vs Equality	6. Legality vs Truth
7. Vengeance vs Justice	8. Self Love vs Universal Love
9. Pride vs Humility	10. Prayer Audible vs Silent
11. Forgiveness	12. Fasting vs Sincerity
13. Riches vs Heart	14. Eye Dual vs Single
15. Two Masters vs One	16. Selfish vs Selfless
17. Judging vs Not	18. Wild vs Aware
19. Wants vs Needs	20. Golden Rule
21. Narrow Way	22. False Prophets
23. Will of God	24. House upon Sand vs Rock

III) Praise & Salvation (Growth & Identity)
Vision Seven

(find in your Bible *these words* see Rev. 21:12–14)
twelve gates . . . twelve foundations ~Praise & Salvation

Praise & Salvation surround the Holy City. "*Violence shall no more be heard in thy land, wasting nor destruction within thy borders; but thou shalt call thy walls Salvation and thy gates Praise*" *(Isaiah 60:18)*.

Day three of seven from Genesis, Elohim creates forms of intelligence, substance, and life . . . and it was good (Genesis 1:10–13). Growth and identity express equally praise and salvation as well as the nature/name of God. Nature in human form like grass, herb, tree hint at humility, supply, fruitage, life, etc.

* Regarding the creation stories of Genesis: Day three of seven corresponds to the Adam & Eve story and the mortal garden, the Eden tree of the knowledge of good and evil; where mortal man can become a God (Genesis 3:22). Day three corresponds to Noah's Ark of safety, made of gopher wood (Genesis 6:14). (Note Christ Jesus rose on the third day after being crucified on a wooden cross—a different kind of ark).

These *twelve gates . . . twelve foundations*, which parallel the twenty-four elders of vision one, can also reflect a matrix of the three creation stories (see Genesis chapter one, two, and six).

chapter one	chapter two	chapter six
1. Holy State	9. Corporeal State	17. Moral State
2. Light	10. Mist	18. Grace
3. Heaven	11. Dust	19. Flood
4. Nature	12. G&E Tree	20. Gofer Ark
5. Seasons	13. Finite Rivers	21. Wind
6. Creatures	14. Prey/Predators	22. Dove
7. Male/Female	15. Eve from Adam	23. Two-by-two
8. Sanctified	16. Temptation/Curse	24. Covenant

IVa) Lamp's Light (Will Done)
Vision One

(find in your Bible *these words* see Rev. 4:5, 6)
lamps of fire burning ~Lamp's Light

Lamp's Light is likened to borrowed light from the Divine energy source. *"Thy word is a lamp unto my feet, and a light unto my path." (Psalm 119:105).* Notice a lamp over a street guides, and *lamps of fire burning* imply safety. *"The Lord is my light and my salvation." (Psalm 27:1).*

This lamp of seven lights is coincident with the seven Spirits of God, traditionally from Isaiah 11:1–2: wisdom, understanding, counsel, fortitude, knowledge, piety, reverence. Here is no darkness, doubt, fear, nor ignorance, hatred, greed, inhumanity.

Likewise, *"Thine is the kingdom, O Lord, and thou art exalted as head above all." (I Chronicles 29:11).* Jesus Christ reveals an elevated mindset of the lamp's light when he said in the Lord's Prayer, *"Thy Kingdom come, Thy will be done."*

Divine light and borrowed light are noumenon and phenomenon. They are coincident, as God is reflected by all of creation. So as one, all are under the same Supreme will.

The Divine will, is likened to God's plan or mighty counsel. *"Many are the plans in the mind of a man, but it is the purpose of the Lord that will stand." (Proverbs 19:21).*

A sea of glass in the heavens spreads this holy kingdom's influence across the universe. *"Hast thou with him spread out the sky, which is strong, and as a molten looking glass?" (Job 37:18).*

As prophetic followers, hide not behind a bushel the borrowed light. Keep God's purpose lit to disperse the dark influences.

Influence others only with graceful patience.

IVa) Foursquare Order (Universal Order)
Vision Seven

(find in your Bible *these words* see Rev. 21:15–21)
golden reed to measure ~Foursquare Order

This reed is similar to the rod given a Shepard. This is the *golden reed to measure*. The *city lieth foursquare*, reminiscent of the four ensigns on the cardinal sides of the Tabernacle of Moses.

Day four of seven from Genesis Elohim created seasons . . . and it was good (see Genesis 1:14–18). The four seasons are representative of universal order. In Winter blessings can be quietly appreciated. In Spring there is new planting. In Summer growth abounds. In Autumn there is harvest. *"To every thing there is a season, and a time to every purpose under the heaven:"* (Ecclesiastes 3:1).

What of the mental dimensions of the infinitesimal and the infinite? The four and twenty precious jewels: *all manner of precious stones* (twelve), and *twelve pearls* again represent the gates and foundations mentioned earlier. *"And they shall be mine, saith the LORD of hosts, in that day when I make up my jewels; and I will spare them"* (Malachi 3:17). *"And they blessed Rebekah, and said unto her, Thou art our sister, be thou the mother of thousands of millions, and let thy seed possess the gate of those which hate them"* (Genesis 24:60).

* Regarding the creation stories of Genesis: Day four of seven corresponds to the Adam & Eve story and finiteness; for the four rivers mark cardinal limits or boundaries (Genesis 2:10–14). The four directional winds in the Noah & Ark story are less physical. The Symbolic moral winds blow across rigid boarders, and pass over the earth to mitigate the flood; that moral regenerative response to corporeality is no longer needed (Genesis 8:1).

Comfort others by sharing a more orderly life.

IVb) Four Ensigns (Earth & Heaven)
Vision One

(find in your Bible *these words* see Rev. 4:6–11)
four beasts ~Four Ensigns

Surrounding the Tabernacle in Exodus, the twelve tribes camped. They camped along the four cardinal directions: north, south, east, and west. Each group of three pitched a single symbolic ensign—a facial symbol sewn on a flag. West was the Ox flag for Ephraim, East was the Lion flag for Judah, South was the face of a Man for Reuben, and North was the Eagle flag for Dan. Scholars agree these four ensigns or standards are represented by the *four beasts* of Revelation. So these four beasts are metaphorically represented as an Ox, Lion, Man, and Eagle.

Isaiah also describes the beasts, *each of them six wings*, "*each one had six wings; with twain he covered his face, and with twain he covered his feet, and with twain he did fly.*" *(Isaiah 6:2)*. Consider that two wings protect angelic thoughts (the ideal); two wings govern angelic actions (upon earth); and the remaining two wings commune (with heaven). Thereby a coincident state of ideal being exists between heaven and earth. *"for the LORD your God, he is God in heaven above, and in earth beneath."* *(Joshua 2:11)*.

Likewise Jesus Christ reveals an elevated mindset of this coincident when he said in the Lord's Prayer, *"In earth as it is in heaven."*

The angelic winged foursome, along with *the four and twenty elders*, offer *glory and honour* to the Holy and Almighty. So for more harmony, give glory and honor in daily life.

More will be said of these four ensigns when later discussing the four horsemen of the apocalypse.

IVb) Glory's Light (Universe Coincident)
Vision Seven

(find in your Bible *these words* see Rev. 21:22–25)
glory . . . did lighten it ~Glory's Light

"*Glorious things are spoken of thee, O city of God.*" *(Psalm 87:3)*. Glory can be symbolized by the sun, moon, stars, of the fourth day from Genesis (Genesis 1:16). "*let them that love him be as the sun when he goeth forth in his might*" *(Deuteronomy 6:4)*. Even a candle can symbolize glory. "*For thou wilt light my candle: the Lord my God will enlighten my darkness.*" *(Psalm 18:28)*. Was not glory symbolized by a burning bush before Moses? "*And the angel of the Lord appeared unto him in a flame of fire out of the midst of a bush:*" *(Exodus 3:2)*.

These objects are of reflected light, or borrowed light, where *glory . . . did lighten it*. In metaphysics there is only one God light source, yet reflected by an infinite variety of forms. "*The sun shall be no more thy light by day; neither for brightness shall the moon give light unto thee: but the Lord shall be unto thee an everlasting light, and thy God thy glory.*" *(Isaiah 60:19)*. Here there is no night, blindness, nor tempest.

This borrowed light of Heaven shines on Earth. From cause to effect is the light of heaven and earth coincident. In the heart of the nations that are saved in this coincident, *shall walk in the light of it*. "*I and my Father (effect and cause) are one.*" *(John 10:30)*. "*And the glory which thou gavest me I have given them;*" *(John 17:22)*.

Comfort others, and thereby the nations, by sharing more of Glory's light.

V) Showbread (Daily Bread)
Vision One

(find in your Bible *these words* see Rev. 5:1–5)
book ~Showbread

How is a book like the Tabernacle's table of showbread? Later in Revelation it states regarding eating a book, *"Take it, and eat it up;"* Ezekiel 3:3 says, *"eat this scroll I am giving you and fill your stomach with it."*

Partaking of *book* or bread are alike in that angelic inspiration feeds and sustains mentally. Inspiration can improve any day, and being inspired daily is the hope of many a hungry heart.

Likewise, Jesus Christ reveals an elevated mindset of bread and wine when he said in the Lord's Prayer, *"Give us this day, our daily Bread."*

Traditionally the table held two plates of unleavened bread, along with pitchers for the pouring out of the wine. Similarly in the New Testament Christ Jesus shared bread and wine with his disciples in communion. This was a sad supper. But *weep not.* The Lord again fed the disciples in the morning hours on the shore of the Galilean sea, proving that the cross cannot harm. *"For the bread of God is he which cometh down from heaven, and giveth life unto the world." (John 6:33).*

Feast upon that inspiration which makes life more fulfilling.

V) Book of Life (Angelic Sustenance)
Vision Seven

(find in your Bible *these words* see Rev. 21:26, 27)
book of life ~Angelic Sustenance

Glory and honour only shall be allowed in the Holy City. Such inspiration feeds and sustains. No mortal messages shall enter consciousness. Thoughts that defileth or maketh a lie in no wise shall enter. Only holy messages of substance enter and become the inspired words of the *book of life*.

Day five of seven from Genesis Elohim unfolds angelic messengers—living, moving, conscious symbols of the Divine . . . and it was good (Genesis 1:20, 21). *"Ask now the beasts, and they shall teach thee; and the fouls of the air, and they shall tell thee: Or speak to the earth, and it shall teach thee: and the fishes of the sea shall declare unto thee." (Job 12:7–8).*

Only living, moving, conscious messengers of the Divine can enter metaphysical being. With mental wings they swiftly deliver glory and honor. All of God's gentle creatures dwell in harmony. *"The wolf also shall dwell with the lamb, and the leopard shall lie down with the kid; and the calf and the young lion and the fatling together; and a little child shall lead them." (Isaiah 11:6).*

* Regarding the creation stories of Genesis: Day five of seven corresponds to the Adam & Eve story with naming the prey and predator. This is survival of the fittest, as physical science teaches (Genesis 2:19). Correspondingly in the Noah story is the dove (Genesis 8:8–13). (Note the symbolic dove at Jesus' baptism in Luke 3:22).

God's creatures are like angelic sustenance. *"And they shall no more be a prey to the heathen, neither shall the beast of the land devour them; but they shall dwell safely, and none shall make them afraid." (Ezekiel 34:28).*

Become angelic and sustain others.

VI) Laver of Water (Forgiveness)
Vision One

(find in your Bible *these words* see Rev. 5:6–10)
by thy blood ~Laver for cleansing

Water filled the brazen laver, and anciently was used by the priesthood in washing their hands. In modern times lavers are also used for purposes of baptism. Blood, like water, fills a similar purpose; *by thy blood*. "In Him we have redemption through His blood, the forgiveness of our trespasses." (Ephesians 1:7).

Jesus Christ reveals an elevated mindset of the Laver of water for cleansing when he said, *"Forgive us our debts as we forgive our debtors."* This is reminiscent of the "golden rule."

Forgiveness, mental ablution, is paramount in daily life. Even under dire circumstances, feeling like one is upon a cross, *for thou wast slain*, still all are taught to forgive. *"Then said Jesus, (upon the cross) Father, forgive them"* (Luke 23:34).

In mirrored form, the forgiver is blessed as much or more than the forgiven. *"if anyone is in (or forgives like) Christ, the new creation has come: The old has gone, the new is here."* (II Corinthians 5:17).

Daily, let us wash away old attitudes; and be baptized with a renewed consciousness that embraces God's grace.

VI) Water of Life (Pure Offspring)
Vision Seven

(find in your Bible *these words* see Rev. 22:1)
water of life ~Pure Offspring

The *water of life,* clear as crystal as purity of thought, flows from the sons and daughters of God. In crystal form the *pure* in heart reflect clear perfection. Impurity, or likewise any bad habit, does not belong to God's offspring. Any conscientious worker can prove this, by removing a bad habit from thought and deed. Jesus saw Mary Magdalene's contrition, which allowed her to be a loyal follower.

Day six of seven from Genesis Elohim unfolds male and female (Genesis 1:27). In this first chapter of Genesis is the immortal perfect offspring of the Divine. *"For in him we live, and move, and have our being; as certain also of your own poets have said, For we are also his offspring." (Acts 17:28).* God's offspring also reflect dominion, not limitation. Inventiveness eternally reveals the Maker's limitless nature.

* Regarding the creation stories of Genesis: Day sixth of seven corresponds to the Adam & Eve story and their offspring, brother killing brother (Genesis 4:8). Also the mortal realm, not the enlightened realm, is where there is not always a proper union of male and female. Here purity is bastardized and adulterated. Here are the lost sheep. *"He that giveth unto the poor shall not lack: but he that hideth his eyes shall have many a curse." (Proverbs28:27).* In the Noah story animals are gathered *"the male and his female" (Genesis 7:2);* as if to say that the morality of male and female leads to harmony and upholds the species. Also Noah's descendants were morally reminded to help the helpless. *"Whoso stoppeth his ears at the cry of the poor, he also shall cry himself, but shall not be heard." (Proverbs 21:13).*

Serve one another and employ inventiveness over limitations to demonstrate neighborly unadulterated love; *"so we, being many, are one body in Christ, and every one members one of another." (Romans 12:5).*

Let us proceed with waters (ideas) of purity in mind and body. *"Christ shall be magnified in my body," (Philippians 1:20).*

VII) Altar of Sacrifice (Deliverance)
Vision One

(find in your Bible *these words* see Rev. 5:11, 12)
Worthy is the Lamb that was slain ~Altar of Sacrifice

The brazen altar of sacrifice is the station where the people brought a live animal as a sin offering to God. The term "sacrificial lamb" and "scapegoat" came from this ancient practice. However, *"sacrifice and offering thou didst not desire; mine ears hast thou opened: burnt offering and sin offering hast thou not required." (Psalm 40:6)*. Instead of a sin offering, obedience to God is preferred. The ritual of the sin offering displayed that temptation prevailed, for temptations come easily to those that are disobedient. Therefore be not lead into temptation through obedience to the deliverer.

Likewise, Jesus Christ, the Lamb of God, *Worthy is the Lamb that was slain*, reveals an elevated mindset of the altar of sacrifice when he said in the Lord's Prayer, *"Lead us not into temptation, but deliver us from evil."*

Therefore bring to the altar obedience, and be delivered from temptation. *"Know ye not, that to whom ye yield yourselves servants to obey, his servants ye are to whom ye obey; whether of sin unto death, or of obedience unto righteousness?" (Romans 6:16)*.

Whoever gratefully obeys the Divine is worthy and receives untold benedictions in daily life. Delivered from evil, the obedient become worthy to receive:

- *power*
- *riches*
- *wisdom*
- *strength*
- *honor*
- *glory*
- *blessing*

VII) Tree of Life (Sanctification)
Vision Seven

(find in your Bible *these words* see Rev. 22:2)
the tree of life ~Sanctification

In spiritual paradise all is sanctified. *"And God blessed the seventh day, and sanctified it:" (Genesis 2:3)*.

The tree of life symbolizes a spiritual ancestral tree, where everyone belongs to a branch. The universal family is one, and sanctified. *"I am the vine, ye are the branches: He that abideth in me, and I in him, the same bringeth forth much fruit: for without me ye can do nothing." (John 15:5)*.

This spiritual tree can only house spiritual growth and fruit. Like always produces like. *"Can the fig tree, my brethren, bear olive berries? either a vine, figs? so can no fountain both yield salt water and fresh." (James 3:12)*.

Good can never produce evil. Innocence is the counter-fact to guilt. *"And every man that striveth for the mastery is temperate in all things." (I Corinthians 9:25)*. On the other hand temptation, or the belief in the separation of God & Offspring, leads away from sanctification. Giving in to temptation, the antipode of atonement, is like abandoning growth. *"And when he saw a fig tree in the way, he came to it, and found nothing thereon, . . . And presently the fig tree withered away." (Matthew 21:19)*.

* Regarding the creation stories of Genesis: Day seven of seven corresponds to the Adam & Eve story and the tempting fruit from the tree of physicality (Genesis 3:4–8). Likewise what tempted Noah was morality's wine, which may not of itself be wrong, however an excess brings shame (Genesis 9:20, 21).

Let us partake of the tree of life and demonstrate holiness. Beholding the tree of life the cross cannot prevent us from obtaining resurrection or ascension. Let us demonstrate a sanctified paradise where all bear good fruit. Salvation then becomes sanctified. *"God hath from the beginning chosen you to salvation through sanctification" (II Thessalonians 2:13)*.

Sanctify and bless the neighbors of the branches.

(interlude—for thine is the kingdom . . .)
Vision One

(find in your Bible *these words* see Rev. 5:13)
Blessing, and honour, and glory, and power

From the Lord's Prayer, *"For thine is the kingdom, and the power, and the glory, for ever."* Interestingly many Bible scholars believe this last part of the Lord's Prayer was not part of the original. No matter, cherish and practice the intent of the Lord's Prayer and fulfill all seven stations of Moses' Tabernacle, with benedictions and blessings flowing to meet the needs of all mankind. Yet this beautiful summary corresponds to verses from Revelation herein:

- *blessing*
- *honour*
- *glory*
- *power*

So ends vision one. Notice how vision one easily parallels vision seven.

(interlude—which bare . . .)
Vision Seven

(find in your Bible *these words* see Rev. 22:2)
which bare twelve [manner] of fruits

Galatians 5:22–23 addresses this *which bare twelve [manner] of fruits*:

- *charity, joy, peace, patience,*
- *kindness, goodness, forbearance, mildness,*
- *faith, modesty, self-control, chastity.*

So ends vision seven. Notice how vision seven easily parallels vision one.

Vision One

Summation

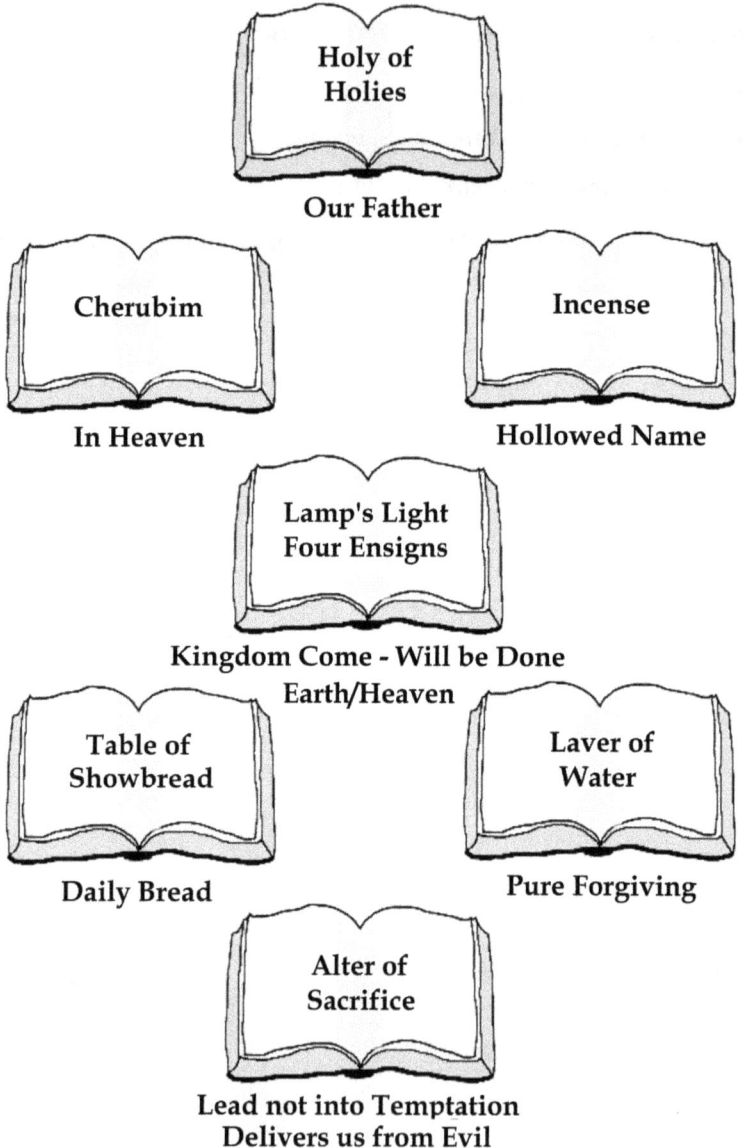

Vision Seven
Summation

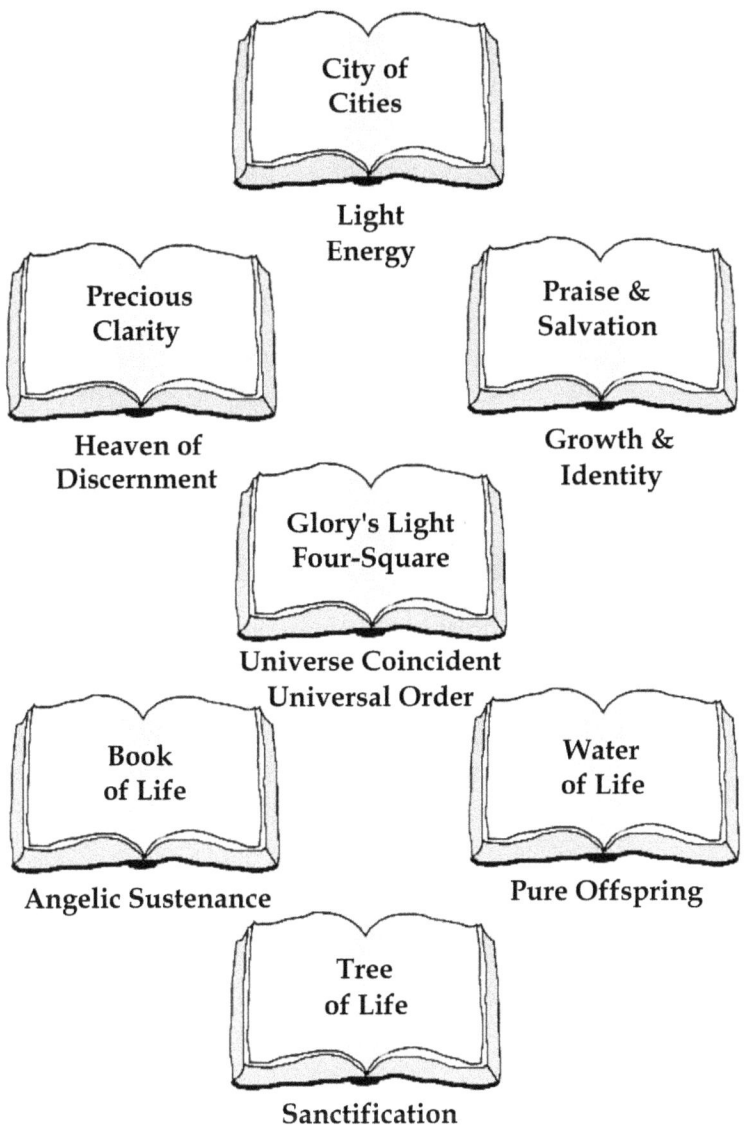

Vision Two

Preview

*He maketh me to lie down in green pastures:
he leadeth me beside the still waters.*

(PSALM 23)

Four angelic ensigns lead to *green pastures and still waters*, and silence the four horsemen of evil:

    I)—White Horse of Deception
    silenced by Unpretentious Ox

    II)—Red Horse of Wrath
    silenced by Dignified Lion

    III)—Black Horse of Greed
    silenced by Generous Man

    IV)—Pale Horse of False Science
    silenced by Perceptive Eagle

(interlude) four horsemen impotent

—these four issues solved
the remaining three become possible.

    V)—Persistence
    silences desertion

    VI)—Repentance
    silences concealment

(interlude) seven glories for servants

    VII)—All Things Calm
    silences evil

Vision Six

Preview

surely goodness & mercy shall follow me
all the days of my life.
(PSALM 23)

Four incorporeal ensigns follow with goodness *and mercy*,
and sing the four songs of selfless love:

> I)—Unpretentious Ox
> praises salvation: Hallelujah

> II)—Dignified Lion
> praises glory: Hallelujah

> III)—Ideal-Man
> praises honor: Hallelujah

> IV)—Perceptive Eagle
> praises power: Hallelujah

(interlude) four ensigns omnipotent

—these four issues solved,
the remaining three become possible:

> V)—Marriage Feast
> praises natural union

> VI)—True & Faithful
> praises the dual witnesses

(interlude) seven dooms for evildoers

> VII)—All Things New
> praises renewal

*Vision Two

Seals Removed (Rev. 6:1—8:1)

He maketh me to lie down in green pastures:
he leadeth me beside the still waters.

(PSALM 23:2)

(find in your Bible *these words* see Rev. 5:14, 6:1)
The Lamb opened one of the seals ~Seals Unraveling

Simply put, the seven seals try to hide or constrict Revelation. Whereas, *The Lamb opened one of the seals*. The Lamb's seven-fold counter-facts remove or unravel these seals to reveal hieroglyphs of being.

First *four beasts* worshiping the Divine appear. These four counter-facts shall unmask the first four seals—the *four horsemen of the apocalypse*—for which voluminous amounts have been written.

Basically the horsemen come to exemplify the temporality of evil. The eternity of good will rise with the counter-facts—the four beasts. These four counter-facts or holy ensigns (the main four symbolic flags of the twelve tribes) surround the Tabernacle of Moses and are camped toward the north, east, west, and south.

After the four horsemen, three more seals follow. Howbeit, counter-facts will also champion these modes. Finally the conclusion becomes evident—evil shall be silenced.

* Regarding Matthew chapter 24: Many have found that the symbolic meaning of vision two closely parallels this chapter. The beginning question is, *"as he sat upon the mount of Olives, the disciples came unto him privately, saying, Tell us, when shall these things be? and what shall be the sign of thy coming (revealing immortal harmony), and of the end of the world (ending mortal suffering)?"* (Matthew. 24:3). Note that a continuation from Matthew chapter 24 will be quoted in all seven sections of this vision.

The following pages provide a quick overview of vision two.

*Vision Six

Goodness Sung (Rev. 19:1—21:8)

*surely goodness & mercy shall follow me
all the days of my life.*

(PSALM 23)

(find in your Bible *these words* see Rev. 19:1)
A great voice of much people in heaven ~Voices Singing

Here there is no constriction. Goodness is sung freely. *A great voice of much people in heaven* sing *Alleluia; Salvation, and glory, and honour, and power.*

As mortal beliefs are silenced, immortal facts can be sung. Utilize this principle. Sing hymns of praise and blessings often. "*Bless the Lord, O my soul, and forget not all his benefits: Who forgiveth all thine iniquities; who healeth all thy diseases; Who redeemeth thy life from destruction; who crowneth thee with lovingkindness and tender mercies;*" (Psalm 103).

In vision two the sequence of four evil horsemen is followed by three woes. Correspondingly in this sixth vision four alleluias in song are followed by three blessings. Combined, vision two and sixth lead to new things. "*Therefore if any man be in Christ, he is a new creature: old things are passed away; behold, all things are become new.*" (II Corinthians 5:17).

Hymns of praise are called forth throughout the Bible. When faced with overwhelming odds, faithful song won the battle described by II Chronicles:20. Amidst the battle, "he appointed singers." Hymns also remove fear. "*Be not afraid nor dismayed by reason of this great multitude; for the battle is no yours, but God's. Ye shall not need to fight in this battle, . . . stand ye still, and see the salvation of the lord . . .*" (II Chronicles 20:15,17).

The following pages provide a quick overview of vision six.

I) Horse of Deception vs Unpretentious Ox
Vision Two

(find in your Bible *these words* see Rev. 6:1, 2)
white horse ~Deception

White is usually the symbol for innocence. Yet the opposite rides into consciousness. Instead of innocence is deception. The rider of the *white horse* also wears a pretentious *crown*.

* Regarding Matthew chapter 24: *"And Jesus answered and said unto them, Take heed that no man deceive you. For many shall come in my name, saying, I am Christ; and shall deceive many." (Matthew 24:4, 5)*. Note the word, deceive.

Remember, there were four ensigns (flags), one for each cardinal direction. Taken in order, the first counter-fact represents the Ox, *one of the four beasts*. So the horseman upon the white horse is an antipode of the Ox. The Ox exposes the self-destructive force of deception.

Oxen are like steady resolve, bearing burdens under the yoke with longsuffering patience. *"Take my yoke upon you, and learn from me, for I am gentle and lowly in heart, and you will find rest for your souls." (Matthew 11:29)*. The Ox is unpretentious. So the unpretentious is the symbol of the Ox. The Ox deceives no one. Do not pretend to be something thou are not. *"they bend their tongues like their bow for lies: . . . one speaketh peaceably to his neighbour with his mouth, but in heart he layeth his wait." (Jeremiah 9:3,8)*.

The Word cannot be silenced. Instead the Word silences evil. In like manner in this scene the guileless and unpretentious Oxen thought silences deception. So study, contemplate, and practice being unpretentious in daily life. Fame is not of itself wrong, but be cautious of any pride of fame.

I) Alleluia
Vision Six

(find in your Bible *these words* see Rev. 19:2)
Alleluia ~Oxen Singing

"That our oxen may be strong to labour;
that there be no breaking in, nor going out;
that there be no complaining in our streets.
Happy is that people, that is in such a case:"
(Ps. 144:14, 15).

"Take my yoke upon you, and learn of me;
for I am meek and lowly in heart:
and ye shall find rest unto your souls.
For my yoke is easy, and my burden is light."
(Matthew 11:29, 30).

II) Horse of Wrath vs Dignified Lion
Vision Two

(find in your Bible *these words* see Rev. 6:3, 4)
horse [that was] red ~Wrath

Red is usually the symbol for blood sacrifice. Yet the opposite rides into consciousness. Instead of dignity in atonement there is wrath. The rider of the *red horse* carries a *great sword* for slaughter.

* Regarding Matthew chapter 24: *"And ye shall hear of wars and rumours of wars: see that ye be not troubled: for all these things must come to pass, but the end is not yet." (Matthew 24:6)*. Note the word, wars.

Also in this scene is the *second beast*. In order of the Tabernacle ensigns the second beast is the Lion. So the horseman upon the red horse is an antipode of the Lion. The Lion exposes the self-destructive force of wrath and wars.

Lions are bold and courageous, even a symbol of honorable kingship. *"the righteous are bold as a lion." (Proverbs 28:1)*. The Lion is dignified. So dignity is a symbol for the Lion. The Lion has no wrath. Not warring takes courage; warring is cowardice—though this is not taught by the world. *"Let not the mighty man glory in his might." (Jeremiah 9:23)*.

The Christ cannot be silenced. Instead Christ silences evil. In like manner in this scene the dignified and honorable Lion thought silences wrath. So study, contemplate, and practice being dignified in daily life. Power is not of itself wrong, but be cautious of any pride of power.

II) Alleluia
Vision Six

(find in your Bible *these words* see Rev. 19:3)
Alleluia ~Lion Singing

"The wicked flee when no man pursueth:
but the righteous are bold as a lion."
(Prov. 28:1).

"The works of the LORD are great,
sought out of all them
that have pleasure therein.
His work is honourable and glorious:"
(Psalms 111:2, 3).

III) Horse of Greed vs Generous Man
Vision Two

(find in your Bible *these words* see Rev. 6:5, 6)
black horse ~Greed

Black in finances indicates accurate and fair accounting. Yet the opposite rides into consciousness. Instead of generosity is greed. The rider of the *black horse* carries a *pair of balances* in his hand marked for unfair trade amongst the nations.

* Regarding Matthew chapter 24: *"For nation shall rise against nation, and kingdom against kingdom: and there shall be famines," (Matthew 24:7).* Note the word, famines.

Also in this scene is the *third beast*. In order of the Tabernacle ensigns the third beast is the generous man, or New-Man. So the horseman upon the black horse is an antipode of the New-Man. *"Let not the rich man glory in his riches." (Jeremiah 9:23).* The New-Man exposes the self-destructive force of greed.

Men can be generous in commerce and still be successful. *"Incline my heart to your testimonies, and not to selfish gain!" (Psalm 119:36).* *"Whoever is generous to the poor lends to the Lord, and he will repay him for his deed." (Proverbs 19:17).* So generosity is a symbol for the New-Man. This being has no greed. Profit is for both parties—though this is not taught by the world.

The prayerful servants in patient service cannot be silenced. Instead generosity in service silences evil. In like manner in this scene the generous thought silences greed. So study, contemplate, and practice being generous in daily life. Wealth is not of itself wrong, but be cautious of any pride of wealth.

III) Alleluia
Vision Six

(find in your Bible *these words* see Rev. 19:4)
Alleluia ~New-Man Singing

*"Lie not one to another, seeing that ye
have put off the old man with his deeds;
And have put on the new man,
which is renewed in knowledge
after the image of him that created him:"*
(Col. 3:9, 10).

*"Put on the new man, which after God is created
in righteousness and true holiness."*
(Ephesians 4:24).

IV) Horse of Pseudo Science vs Perceptive Eagle
Vision Two

(find in your Bible *these words* see Rev. 6:7, 8)
pale horse ~Ptolemaic Effect

Pale is the color nearing death. The horseman's name is also death. The rider of the *pale horse* drags *hell* behind him.

* Regarding Matthew chapter 24: "*and pestilences, and earthquakes, in divers places.*" *(Matthew 24:7)*. Note the words, pestilences and earthquakes.

Also in this scene is the *fourth beast*. In order of the Tabernacle ensigns, the forth beast is the Eagle. So the horseman upon the pale horse is an antipode of the Eagle. "*they that wait (focus) upon the Lord shall renew their strength; they shall mount up with wings as eagles;*" *(Isaiah 40:31)*. The Eagle exposes the self-destructive force of pseudo science.

The perception of an Eagle is reasoning above temporal science. "*Wherever the body (Christ) is, there the eagles will be gathered together.*" *(Luke 17:37)*. Reasoning is free from ptolemaic empirical science and pseudo *ologies* which all eventually succumb to a pale death. Ptolemy's theory, that the earth was the center of the solar system, lasted as long as 1300 years. Interestingly injecting or digesting harmful chemicals is medically acknowledged today to bring health or relaxation. Yet there is a demand for clean air and clean water—to keep the earth-body pure!

Mental quackery drags behind the pale horse. Thus wasting time in self-servicing endeavors, or being influenced by others is hypnosis, leading eventually to cerebral earthquakes. "*Let not the wise man glory in his wisdom.*" *(Jeremiah 9:23)*.

Perceptive rationality opposes the ever changing theories of atomics and biologics that foster fear or false belief. Thus the perceptive Eagle devours serpents of unnatural and harmful promises. Temporal principles pale in comparison to holy principle.

The Holy Spirit cannot forever be silenced. Instead the Holy Spirit silences imitative pseudo science. Knowledge is not of itself wrong, but be cautious of any pride of knowledge.

IV) Alleluia
Vision Six

(find in your Bible *these words* see Rev. 19:5, 6)
Alleluia ~Eagle Singing

*"they that wait upon the Lord
shall renew their strength;
they shall mount up with wings as eagles;
they shall run, and not be weary;
and they shall walk, and not faint."*
(Isa. 40:31).

*"He shall cover thee with his feathers,
and under his wings shalt thou trust:"*
(Psalms 91:4)

(interlude—horsemen impotent)
Vision Two

(find in your Bible *these words* see Rev. 6:8)
power . . . over the fourth part of the earth

* Regarding Matthew chapter 24: *"All these are the beginning of sorrows." (Matthew 24:8).* Evil deeds bring with it sorrow to itself.

These four horsemen have only partial temporary power, *power . . . over the fourth part of the earth*. They do not have power over the faithful in the world. Recklessness destroys itself, wherever it resides.

Holy power belongs to God's four ensigns. Omnipotence and omnipresence protects the upright, wherever they reside.

Wonderfully discovered likenesses:

The *Word*, likened to the unpretentious Ox,
silences deception riding upon a white horse,
and cautions against pride of fame.

The *Christ*, likened to the dignified Lion,
silences wrath riding upon a red horse,
and cautions against pride of power.

The *Servant*, likened to the generous Man,
silences greed riding upon a black horse,
and cautions against pride of wealth.

The *Holy Spirit*, likened to the perceptive Eagle,
silences pseudo science riding upon a pale horse,
and cautions against pride of knowledge.

(interlude—creator omnipotent)
Vision Six

(find in your Bible *these words* see from Rev. 19:6)
omnipotent

Vision two has an interlude. So too here in vision six. One interlude informs that the four horsemen are impotent. Thereupon the four Hallelujahs are *omnipotent*.

"And he hath put a new song in my mouth" (Psalm 40:3).

Note:
Among scholars
regarding this pairing of the four horsemen
to the four beasts
there is no consistency.

V) Desertion vs Persistence
Vision Two

(find in your Bible *these words* see Rev. 6:9–11)
How long, O Lord ~Desertion

* Regarding Matthew chapter 24: *"Then shall they deliver you up to be afflicted, and shall kill you: and ye shall be hated of all nations for my name's sake. And then shall many be offended, and shall betray one another, and shall hate one another. And many false prophets shall rise, and shall deceive many. And because iniquity shall abound, the love of many shall wax cold."* (Matthew 24:9–12). The idea of spiritual desertion is the sorest affliction to those that think they are righteous. *"Three men ceased to answer Job, because he was righteous in his own eyes." (Job 31:3; 32:1)*.

Because God always saves the true believers, Jesus Christ is able to show humanity that life is spiritual and eternal, and not comprised of the material body or world. *How long, O Lord*. Asking why one failed to solve a mathematical problem does no good. Instead persist to reapply the basic principles until the solution is found.

Patience is a virtue. So be not discouraged; *rest yet for a little season*. *"But he that shall endure unto the end, the same shall be saved." (Matthew 24:13)*. Persistence, endurance, steadfastness, are the morning meal of Christ at the edge of the Galilean sea.

Endure and persist—follow the Savior.

V) Marriage Feast
Vision Six

(find in your Bible *these words* see Rev. 19:7–10)
marriage supper ~Natural Union

There is a great banquet, a *marriage supper*. Marriage is a sacred mode for demonstrating morality. Unfortunately many do not want to partake of the holy significance of marriage. So marriage is becoming a broken institution, desertion runs ramped. Persistent compromise in the union of two sexes often goes missing. Nature's natural order of procreation is adulterated.

"*And Jesus answered and spake unto them again by parables, and said, The kingdom of heaven is like unto a certain king, which made a marriage for his son, And sent forth his servants to call them that were bidden to the wedding: and they would not come.*" *(Matthew 22:1–3)*.

Beyond corporeal lust, the more elevated moral state awaits to be demonstrated. Then enlightened being announces itself. "*I will betroth thee unto me for ever;*" *(Hosea 2:19)*. In the City of Cities there is spiritual unity. Neither division nor polarization is found therein.

When discouraged and feeling alone, we may think in our ignorance that lone footprints indicate that there is no God. Howbeit, it is God that is carrying us across the wilderness. "*for he hath said, I will never leave thee, nor forsake thee.*" *(Hebrews 13:5)*.

Do not give an excuse when hearing whispers of graceful offerings. Be glad and rejoice to have been invited to join with the Lord.

VI) Concealment vs Repentance
Vision Two

(find in your Bible *these words* see Rev. 6:12–17)
hid themselves ~Concealment

* Regarding Matthew chapter 24: *"Immediately after the tribulation of those days shall: the sun be darkened, and the moon shall not give her light, and the stars shall fall from heaven, and the powers of the heavens shall be shaken:"* (Matthew 24:29). Mortality attempts to conceal wrongdoing.

Some believe that they *hid themselves* by confessing a fault, as though simple confession absolves the wrong. What is required though is penance and regeneration, changing bad habits into good deeds. *"Adam and his wife hid themselves from the presence of the LORD God amongst the trees of the garden."* (Genesis 3:8). Here is the first instance of trying to hide a fault from the Holy One in Heaven. *"There is nothing covered, that shall not be revealed; and hid, that shall not be known"* (Matthew 10:26).

Does civilized law absolve a murderer of the crime if they simply confess their guilt? No. Judicial principle causes the immoral character hardship, until there is evidence of genuine repentance. More than a mere confession, forsaking disgraceful habits and taking up graceful acts is required. Trying to conceal reckless behavior is impossible. Exposing evil is God's law. *"He that covereth his sins shall not prosper: but whoso confesseth and forsaketh them shall have mercy."* (Proverbs 28:13).

Repentance is demonstrated in practice. Probation is proving one has changed while under dire temptation. *"For they being ignorant of God's righteousness, and going about to establish their own righteousness, have not submitted themselves unto the righteousness of God."* (Romans 10:3).

Follow and repent—witness the Savior.

VI) True & Faithful
Vision Six

(find in your Bible *these words* see Rev. 19:11–16)
Faithful and True ~Two Witnesses

Thought and action, if God governed, leads to blessed testimonials. Opposite of the true dual witnesses, are the false witness seen in vision two: these being the beast of the sea and the false prophet. Over-action or under-action are also false witnesses. The two great commandments might be thought of as the two great witnesses, *Faithful and True*.

"Finally, brethren,

whatsoever things are true,
whatsoever things are honest,
whatsoever things are just,
whatsoever things are pure,
whatsoever things are lovely,
whatsoever things are of good report;
if there be any virtue, and if there be any praise,
think on these things"
(Philippians 4:8).

There is much literature debating who are these two witnesses. Are the two witnesses complimentary pieces, the Holy Ghost and the Christ? The Bible links them so. *"Repent, and be baptized every one of you in the name of Jesus Christ for the remission of sins, and ye shall receive the gift of the Holy Ghost." (Acts 2:38).*

Regardless study, contemplate, and practice the aforementioned list of character traits. Let them stand as the most compassionate of motivations and deeds. These shall continually bring more harmony into daily life.

(interlude—glory for servants)
Vision Two

(find in your Bible *these words* see Rev. 7:1–3)
hurt not

There is no need or requirement for vengeance. Those who do not seek vengeance or retribution shall be protected. They shall *hurt not* even their enemy. Such servants receive glory.

The following seven sections illustrate there are no cultural or ethnical restrictions on who can follow after good, *till we have sealed the servants*. "... *whether we be Jews or Gentiles, whether we be bond or free;*" (I Corinthians 12:13). In addition, each of the following sections amply glory for those who *serve* the Divine.

I heard the number of them which were sealed.

(interlude—doom for evildoers)
Vision Six

(find in your Bible *these words* see Rev. 19:17)
the supper

This interlude is liken to vision two, but instead of glory for servants, this vision is doom for evildoers. This interlude is not a benediction, and *the supper* is not a hallowed event. It is nothing like a marriage feast. Here is doom for the evildoers, a meal to devour all evil traits. Again evil is seen again to be self-destroyed; T*hat ye may eat the flesh.*

Who are evildoers? They are certainly not those that obey Elohim. They are not even those that struggle with morality. The evildoers are the actors of disobedience. They are not person, but the actions of the ignorant. Disobedience are deeds that have no grace in them. Consider the seven deadly sins. These activities are the evildoers. Teach the ignorant the ways of the Lord.

Separate the evil deeds from the individual. Those that act out evil are under hypnotic influence. Fortunately anyone can put off the old man by removing themselves from evil actions by overcoming the tenacity of hypnotic malicious control.

Never condemn oneself, or another. *"For God sent not his Son into the world to condemn the world; but that the world through him might be saved." (John 3:17).* Instead of condemning oneself, consider probation and overcome. Be more obedient. Gain more confidence in God. *"For if our heart condemn us, God is greater than our heart, and knoweth all things. Beloved, if our heart condemn us not, then have we confidence toward God." (I John 3:20, 21).*

1. glory to a number of followers
Vision Two

(find in your Bible *these words* see Rev. 7:4–8)
number of them

A *number of them* are listed. Many will come from the twelve tribes of Israel. Yet a number implies not all. Note Joseph and Levi replaced Dan and Ephraim, because the latter permitted Jeroboam to set up "Golden Calves" to be worshipped, one at Dan (for the tribe of Dan), and the other at Bethel (for the tribe of Ephraim)—see I Kings 12:25–30.

This interlude contains several more groups of followers besides those that can be numbered, and those that cannot be numbered, i.e., those joined with angels, those purified by tribulation, and those that serve.

2. glory to followers no man could number
Vision Two

(find in your Bible *these words* see Rev. 7:9, 10)
great multitude, which no man could number

A *great multitude, which no man could number.* Japheth, Ishmael, and other ancients also created vast tribes. From these other tribes is even a greater number of true believers.

What is also implied if all these followers are to be sealed servants? They must be ones that can get along with their neighbors. So to be counted as sealed servants with God, have more compassion for fellow beings.

1. doom to fleshly followers
Vision Six

(find in your Bible *these words* see Rev. 19:18)
free and bond, both small and great

Do not be a follower of evil ways and lust of the flesh, though they be *free and bond, both small and great.*

2. doom to those marked by the beast
Vision Six

(find in your Bible *these words* see Rev. 19:19–21)
that had received the mark of the beast

Worship only the Divine good. Keep pure and upright. Unlike they *that had received the mark of the beast.*

3. glory to those joined with angels
Vision Two

(find in your Bible *these words* see Rev. 7:11, 12)
angels stood

Join the followers that support where the *angels stood*. Here is true knowledge and wisdom.

4. glory to those purified by trials
Vision Two

(find in your Bible *these words* see. 7:13, 14)
which came out of great tribulation

There are many followers *which came out of great tribulation*. "*That the trial of your faith, being much more precious than of gold that perisheth, though it be tried with fire, might be found unto praise and honour and glory at the appearing of Jesus Christ:*" *(I Peter 1:7).* Trials are God's benevolence in disguise, teaching His offspring to lean upon the Divine and not the human.

3. doom to the dragon
Vision Six

(find in your Bible *these words* see Rev. 20:1–3)
the bottomless pit

Do not fall into *the bottomless pit* with the dragon. Rise up, and cast away any evil characteristics and practices.

4. doom to the rest of the dead
Vision Six

(find in your Bible *these words* see Rev. 20:4–6)
the rest of the dead

Resurrection is the awaking that evil has no power. The goodness of the Divine has all-power, all-presence. Do no go with the dragon into bottomless pit for a thousand years as do *the rest of the dead*.

5. glory to those that serve
Vision Two

(find in your Bible *these words* see Rev. 7:15)
Serve Him

Service is a holy activity. *Serve Him* by serving others.

6. glory in benediction from the Lamb
Vision Two

(find in your Bible *these words* see Rev. 7:16, 17)
The Lamb

The Lamb will comfort prayerful servants in patient service. They will be hungry for purpose no more. Christ shall feed and lead thy sheep to living waters.

7. glory in benediction from God
Vision Two

(find in your Bible *these words* see Rev. 7:17)
God shall wipe away all tears from their eyes

And for their persistence and repentance *God shall wipe away all tears from their eyes*. How calming is this interlude, knowing goodness and virtue are omnipotent.

5. doom to the last perversion
Vision Six

(find in your Bible *these words* see Rev. 20:7–10)
tormented day and night for ever and ever

The false trinity (devil, beast of the sea, false prophet) have no power. Their power shall dwindle, finding themselves *tormented day and night for ever and ever*. Through torment mortal suggestions, beliefs, and pain shall be burnt up like the chaff. The wheat of metaphysics remains. Understanding, and the existence of good only, can never be perverted.

6. doom to those that fled away.
Vision Six

(find in your Bible *these words* see Rev. 20:11)
fled away

The fleshly earth and heaven of corporeality *fled away* before all powerful and governing Divine. Howbeit the counter-fact to the dragon's world, the spiritual earth and heaven remain forever.

7. doom to those not written in the book of life
Vision Six

(find in your Bible *these words* see Rev. 20:12–15)
not found written in the book of life

To those *not found written in the book of life* are cast with the devil into the lake of fire. Fortunately to servants in service comes the resurrection and ascension, which protects from the suffering of the second death, the complete and total self-annihilation of evil. "*Who shall ascend into the hill of the Lord? or who shall stand in his holy place? He that hath clean hands, and a pure heart; who hath not lifted up his soul unto vanity, nor sworn deceitfully. He shall receive the blessing from the Lord, and righteousness from the God of his salvation*" (Psalm 24:3–5).

VII) All Things Calm
Vision Two

(find in your Bible *these words* see Rev. 8:1)
silence in heaven ~Calm Stillness

Unmasking all seven seals, which attempt to block one's understanding of the Divine, reveals calm spirituality, *silence in heaven*. Thus a great counter-fact is revealed—evil has no true voice. It is illusion, a liar and a lie.

* Regarding Matthew chapter 24: *"And then shall appear the sign of the Son of man in heaven: and then shall all the tribes of the earth mourn, and they shall see the Son of man coming in the clouds of heaven with power and great glory." (Matthew 24:30).*

Power and great glory silences mortal turmoil and selfhood. God is as a "still small voice," yet more powerful than the wind, earthquake, or fire (see I Kings 19:11–13).

Counter-facts that still and silence evil have now been identified in this vision. The seven masks of the liar have been replaced by the seven truth-giving principles.

For more harmony every day, reverse the four horsemen of the apocalypse, and practice the qualities of the "four ensigns" of the Tabernacle, which *silence* all evil, through the qualities of:

- unpretentiousness
- dignity
- generosity
- perceptivity

So ends vision two. Notice how vision two easily parallels vision six.

VII) All Things New
Vision Six

(find in your Bible *these words* see Rev. 21:1–4)
I make all things new ~Renewal

All things new come into view by exchanging the corporeal for the incorporeal. *"Therefore if any man be in Christ, he is a new creature: old things are passed away; behold, all things are become new"* (II Corinthians 5:17). *"Remember ye not the former things, neither consider the things of old. Behold I will do a new thing;"* (Isaiah 43: 18,19). *"That ye put off concerning the former conversation the old man, which is corrupt according to the deceitful lusts; And be renewed in the spirit of your mind; And that ye put on the new man, which after God is created in righteousness and true holiness"* (Ephesians 4:22–24).

From this *I make all things new* position, hell shall pass away. As it says, *God shall wipe away*:

- *tears*
- *death*
- *sorrow*
- *crying*
- *pain*

So ends vision six. Notice how vision six easily parallels vision two.

Vision Two
Summation

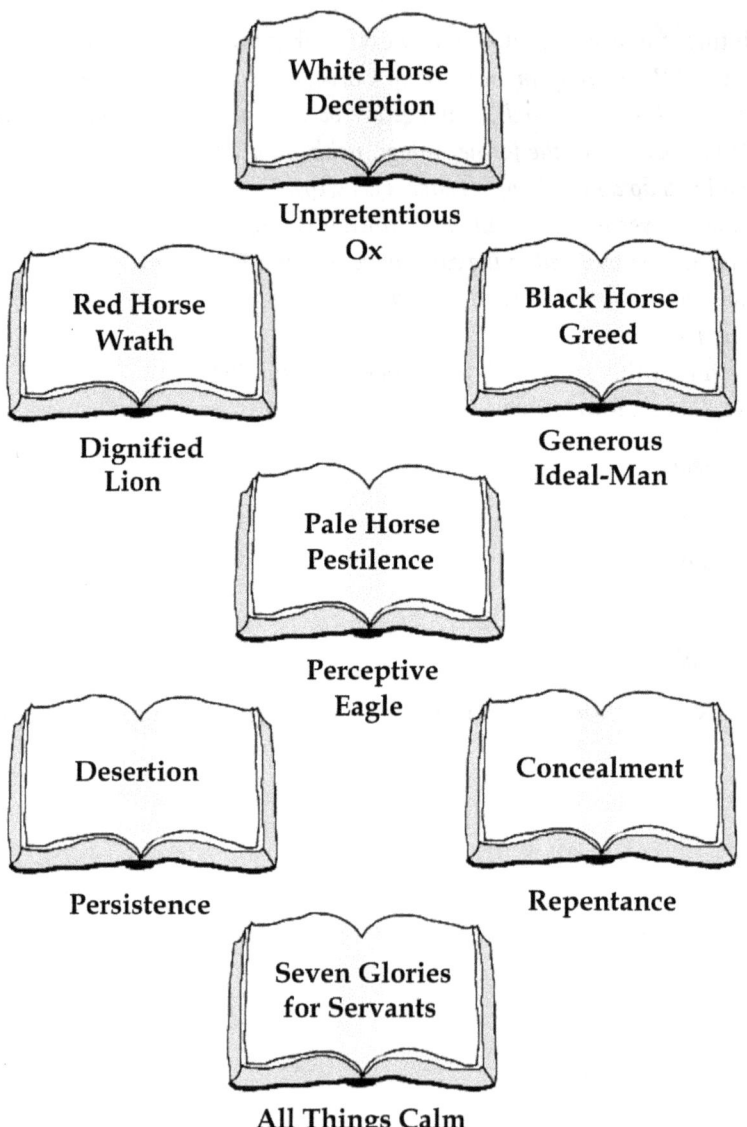

Vision Six

Summation

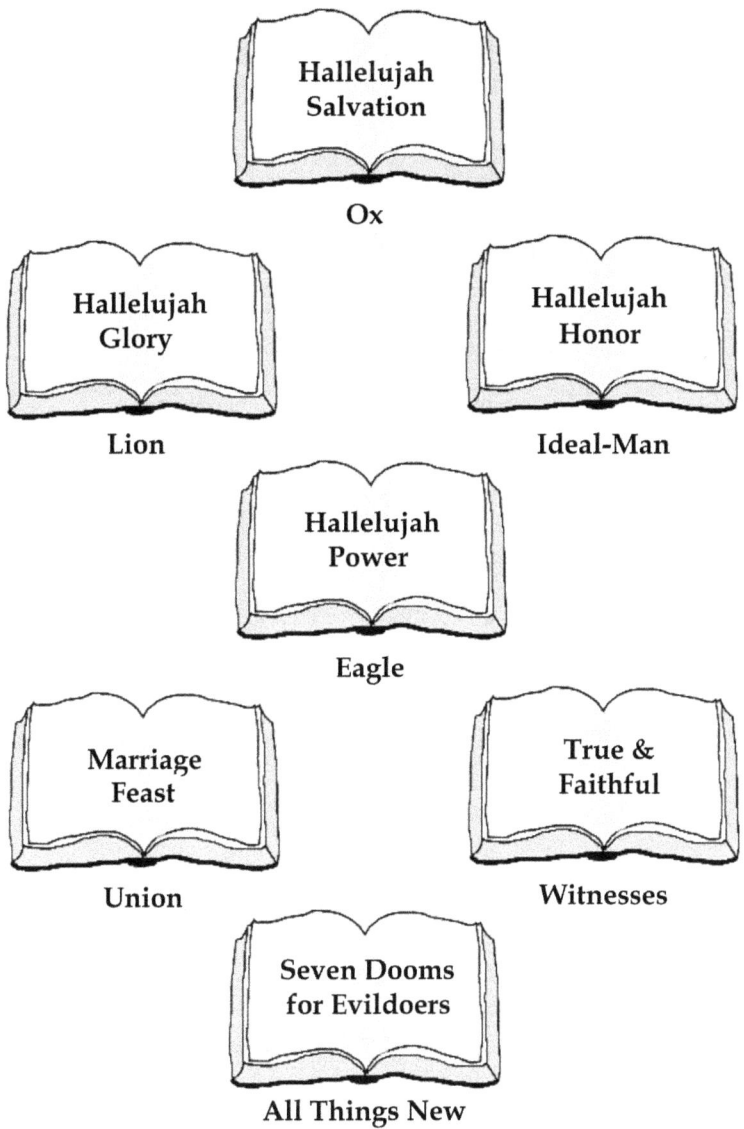

Vision Three

Preview

He restoreth my soul
He leadeth me in paths of righteousness (justice).

(PSALM 23)

Trumpets of *Justice* bring afflictions and woes to the hardheaded:

    I)—Substance; like solidity of Earth must herald Justice

    II)—Intelligence; like fluidity of Sea must herald Justice

    III)—Life Experiences; like extensive Rivers must herald Justice

    IV)—Seasons of Renewal; must herald Justice

    V)—Authority; without Justice is a first woe

    VI)—Human Rights; without Justice is a second woe

(interlude)
True Witnesses
Little-Book, Rod

    VII)—Mercy without Justice is a third woe

(extension)
Virgin:
Clothed with Sun
Enemy of Dragon
Eternal Child to Rule
Dwelling Protected
Sustained

Vision Five

Preview

*Thou anointest my head with oil (mercy)
my cup runneth over*
(PSALM 23)

Cups of *Mercy* bring affliction and woes to the heartless:

    I)—Substance; like Earth solidity, must contain Mercy

    II)—Intelligence; like Sea fluidity, must contain Mercy

    III)—Life Experiences; like Rivers extensive, must contain Mercy

    IV)—Seasons of Renewal; must contain Mercy

    V)—Authority; without Mercy is a woe

    VI)—Human Rights; without Mercy is a woe

(interlude)
False Witnesses
Sea-Beast, False-Prophet

    VII)—Justice without Mercy is a woe

(extension)
Harlot:
Clothed in scarlet
Friend of Dragon
False Kings to Rule
Dwelling Destroyed
Defunct

*Vision Three

Trumpets of Justice (Rev. 8:2—12:6)

He restoreth my soul:
he leadeth me in paths of righteousness (justice).

(PSALM 23:3)

(find in your Bible *these words* see Rev. 8:2–6)
seven trumpets ~Trumpets of Justice

In the New Testament, written in Greek, the word for justice also means righteousness, i.e., translation from Latin, "justice", and the same word translation from German, "righteousness."

Simply put, the *seven trumpets* announce destruction for the unjust. The counter-fact is the incense of praise where the seven trumpets of Justice announce harmony for the just.

First, four parts of nature will be discussed: the earth, sea, rivers, and sky above. Challenges will abound. Counter-facts will reveal harmony. Natural law will become self-evident. Trumpets of justice shall expose corruption, and it destroys itself.

Next three woes will be discussed, for which voluminous amounts have been written. Basically these three come to destroy unholy traits. In summation, *"Woe to the rebellious children, saith the Lord, that take counsel, but not of me."* (Isaiah 30:1).

Consider the trumpets of justice in the story of Joshua chapter six. For seven successive days the trumpets sounded. They did not harm the prayerful, but did cause a woe to the walls of Jericho that fell. The fall of Jericho allowed the tribes to enter the promise land. *"With trumpets and the sound of the horn make a joyful noise before the King, the Lord! . . . He will judge the world with righteousness, and the peoples with equity"* (Psalm 98: 6–9).

For completeness, justice is eternally linked to mercy. *"what does the Lord require of you? To act justly and to love mercy"* (Micah 6:8). The Divine demands a coequal partnership of justice and mercy. Similarly, the Mosaic law partners with Christly love. One without the other is like letting society do anything they want without rules and discipline, or not letting anyone have a second chance to reform.

The following pages provide a quick overview of vision three.

*Vision Five

Cups of Mercy (Rev. 15:1—18:24)

*Thou anointest my head with oil (of Mercy),
my cup runneth over*

(PSALM 23)

(find in your Bible *these words* see Rev. 15:1–8, 16:1)
seven last plagues ~Cups of Mercy

In the New Testament, written in Greek, the word for mercy is "eleos." An English definition for mercy is kindness or good will towards the miserable and afflicted. "*Therefore will I give thanks unto thee, O LORD, . . . Great deliverance giveth he to his king; and sheweth mercy to his anointed, to David, and to his seed for evermore.*" (Psalm 18:49, 50).

Simply put, the *seven last plagues* pour forth destruction upon the merciless, *vials of the wrath of God*. The counter-fact is that seven cups of mercy pour forth harmony upon the merciful. Mercy is also eternally linked to justice, for Christly love partners with the Mosaic law. "*what does the Lord require of you? To act justly and to love mercy*" (Micah 6:8).

First, four parts of nature will be discussed: the earth, sea, rivers, and sky above. Counter-facts will reveal harmony. Natural law will become self-evident. Cups of mercy shall expose mercilessness, and it destroys itself.

Next three more issues will be discussed. Like the three woes of vision three, the woes of vision five come to destroy unholy traits. So, "the wrath of God" spoken of in the Bible is really saying that mercy demands that the unmerciful suffer, and that the counter-fact of this wrath is the mercy of God!

"*When Christ, who is our life, shall appear, then shall ye also appear with him in glory. Mortify therefore your members which are upon the earth; fornication, uncleanness, inordinate affection, evil 'concupiscence,' and covetousness, which is idolatry: For which things' sake the wrath of God cometh on the children of disobedience:*" (Colossians 3:4–6).

The following pages provide a quick overview of vision five.

I) Substance without Justice is consumed
Vision Three

(find in your Bible *these words* see Rev. 8:7)
earth ~Substance

Earth is used here as a symbol of substance. *"I lead in the way of righteousness, in the midst of the paths of judgment: That I may cause those that love me to inherit substance;" (Proverbs 8:20, 21).*

Is substance solely under the control of the material? No. That is why injustice can only destroy a third part.

Justice and substance as spiritual surpass mortality. *"Now faith is the substance of things hoped for, the evidence of things not seen." (Hebrews 11:1).*

I) Substance without Mercy is grievous
Vision Five

(find in your Bible *these words* see Rev. 16:2)
earth ~Substance

Again consider substance as a symbol for the *earth*. Is substance solely under the control of the material? Certainly without mercy the substance of existence is *noisome and grievous sore*. Without mercy and substance one cannot differentiate between the corporeal and the incorporeal.

Consider the substance expressed by a Patriarch. *"Bless, LORD, his substance, and accept the work of his hands: smite through the loins of them that rise against him, and of them that hate him, that they rise not again." (Deuteronomy 33:11)*. Mercy and substance being spiritual surpass mortality.

II) Intelligence without Justice is consumed
Vision Three

(find in your Bible *these words* see Rev. 8:8, 9)
sea ~Intelligence

Sea is used here as a symbol of intelligence. *"the earth shall be full of the knowledge of the LORD, as the waters cover the sea." (Isaiah 11:9).*

Is intelligence solely under the control of the material? No. That is why injustice can only destroy a third part.

Justice and intelligence as spiritual surpass mortality. *"Understanding is a wellspring of life unto him that hath it: but the instruction of fools is folly." (Proverbs 16:22).*

II) Intelligence without Mercy is drowning madness
Vision Five

(find in your Bible *these words* see Rev. 16:3)
sea ~Intelligence

Again consider intelligence as a symbol for the *sea*. Is intelligence solely under the control of the material? Certainly without mercy, intelligence will have *died in the sea*. Without mercy and intelligence one cannot differentiate between fact and fiction.

Consider the intelligence expressed by a Prophet. *"Thus saith the Lord, which maketh a way in the sea, and a path in the mighty waters; Remember ye not the former things, neither consider the things of old. Behold, I will do a new thing;" (Isaiah 43:16, 18, 19)*. Mercy and intelligence being spiritual surpass mortality.

III) Experience without Justice is consumed
Vision Three

(find in your Bible *these words* see Rev. 8:10, 11)
rivers ~Experiences

Rivers are used here as a symbol of experiences. *"as the rivers of water: he turneth it whithersoever he will." (Proverbs 21:1)*.

Is experience solely under the control of the unjust? No. That is why injustice can only destroy a third part. *"There shall no evil happen to the just: but the wicked shall be filled with mischief." (Proverbs 12:21)*.

Justice and experience as spiritual being must surpass mortality. *"I have learned by experience that the Lord hath blessed me . . ." (Genesis 30:27)*.

III) Experience without Mercy is bitter blood to drink
Vision Five

(find in your Bible *these words* see Rev. 16:4–7)
rivers ~Experiences

Again consider experiences as a symbol for the *rivers*. Is experience solely under the control of the merciless? No.

Without mercy in daily experience, men will *shed the blood* of the saintly. Thus we must counter-act with mercy to friends as well as enemies.

Consider the experiences of Jesus the Christ. *"This cup is the new testament in my blood, which is shed for you." (Luke 22:20).*

IV) Seasons without Justice is consumed
Vision Three

(find in your Bible *these words* see Rev. 8:12)
sun, moon, stars ~Seasons

Sun, moon, stars are used here as a symbol of seasons. *"He appointed the moon for seasons: the sun knoweth his going down." (Psalm 104:19)*.

Seasons of ordered renewal are not overruled by mortality. That is why injustice can only temporarily destroy a third part. *"Choosing rather to suffer affliction with the people of God, than to enjoy the pleasures of sin for a season;" (Hebrew 11:25)*.

Justice and seasons as spiritual surpass mortality . . ."*And let us not be weary in well-doing: for in due season we shall reap, if we faint not." (Galatians 6:9)*.

IV) Seasons without Mercy is great heat
Vision Five

(find in your Bible *these words* see Rev. 16:8, 9)
sun ~Seasons

Consider seasons as a symbol for the *sun*. Without mercy of renewal and order all are *scorched with great heat*.

Consider the seasons of Jesus the Christ, who brought a cup of cold water to the thirsty. "*Whosoever shall give to drink unto one of these little ones a cup of cold water only in the name of a disciple, verily I say unto you, he shall in no wise lose his reward.*" (Matthew 10:42).

(interlude—woes)
Vision Three

(find in your Bible *these words* see Rev. 8:13)
woe, woe, woe

After four sections, now cometh three sections, *woe, woe, woe*. Scholarly writing focuses upon these three woes perhaps even more than on the preceding four sections.

"If I be wicked, woe unto me;" (Job 10:15). *"Woe unto them that call evil good, and good evil;" (Isaiah 5:20)*. *"Woe unto him that buildeth his house by unrighteousness," (Jeremiah 22:13)*.

Vision five woes parallel woes of vision three. Still do not fear. These woes destroy only the evil of injustice. Also the woes are transformed by counter-facts where the servants of holy justice:

1. defy oppression,
2. uphold human rights,
3. bless with justice.

(interlude—woes)
Vision Five

(find in your Bible *these words* see Rev. 16:9)
they repented not

As in vision three, so here in this vision, after four sections three sections follow, each with a woe. subcategories regarding justice and mercy parallel one another.

These woes appear, for *they repented not.* "*Repent, and turn yourselves from all your transgressions; so iniquity shall not be your ruin.*" (Ezekiel 18:30).

Still a woe is nothing to fear, no matter how many there be. The counter-fact is that repentance can overcome any woe. Also the woes are transformed by counter-facts where the servants of holy mercy:

1. defy oppression,
2. uphold human rights,
3. bless with mercy.

V) Authority without Justice is a woe
Vision Three

(find in your Bible *these words* see Rev. 9:1–12)
bottomless pit ~Oppression

The first woe to the material world is the *bottomless pit* of oppression. The angel knows far well that ignorance, sin, and fear oppress; while hope, faith, and understanding hold the key and open the door to enlightened authority with justice for all.

Out of the smoke locusts. Locusts were harmful to the Egyptian rulers, a plague from Moses for not being just to Abraham's seed. However, locusts were useful to John the Baptist in feeding him. Here again, woes harm only evil, not the good.

Consider David's lament on authority without justice, *"LORD, thou hast heard the desire of the humble: . . . To judge the fatherless and the oppressed, that the man of the earth may no more oppress." (Psalm 10:17, 18).*

V) Authority without Mercy is a dark pit of pain
Vision Five

(find in your Bible *these words* see Rev. 16:10, 11)
full of darkness ~Oppression

First woe: Is not a kingdom *full of darkness* oppression? In vision three where a star falls from heaven; here in vision five is authority without mercy. Without mercy the world is full of woeful pains and sores. Defying oppression brings light and mercy. *"Ye shall not oppress one another:" (Leviticus 25:14).*

Consider the light of mercy spoken of by Jesus the Christ. *"The light of the body is the eye: therefore when thine eye is single, thy whole body also is full of light; but when thine eye is evil, thy body also is full of darkness." (Luke 11:34).*

VI) Human Rights without Justice is a woe
Vision Three

(find in your Bible *these words* see Rev. 9:13–21)
Euphrates ~Human Rights

The second woe to the material world is inhumane boarders. The Bible tells repeatedly of God's Promised Land, which is boarded by the Nile and *Euphrates* rivers. This covenant or promise includes morality upholding human rights. But historically the physical borders, as well as the mental borders of the people's consciousness, often lacked human rights. See what happens to the loins of pride and inhumanity at the edge of the Euphrates by reading Jeremiah chapter 13. *"This evil people, which refuse to hear my words, which walk in the imagination of their heart, and walk after other gods, to serve them, and to worship them, shall even be as this girdle, which is good for nothing." (Jeremiah 13: 10)*.

Justice demands that human rights be upheld. *"Do we not all have one Father ? Did not one God create us? Why do we profane the covenant of our ancestors by being unfaithful to one another?" (Malachi 2:10)*. This includes equality of the masculine and feminine. They are not separate but compound and complete. Whereas the word sex can imply and degrade into division.

A land without human rights opens one-third of its borders to chaos and plagues. Woe to the worldly who uphold not human rights. *"Woe unto the wicked! it shall be ill with him: . . ." (Isaiah 3:11)*.

VI) Human Rights without Mercy is genocide
Vision Five

(find in your Bible *these words* see Rev. 16:12)
Euphrates ~Human Rights

Second Woe: Again consider human rights as a symbol for the *Euphrates*. Mentally, Babylon resides on one side, and the Promised Land resides on the other. Mercy demands the compound and complete equality of the masculine and feminine. Whereas inhumanity and mercilessness devises division.

The river of human rights without mercy becomes *dried up*. Such condition is a woe, because now the kings of the east (Babylon—symbol for hypocrisy) are prepared to invade. Only human rights with mercy is the catalyst that can prevent the continuing terrorism and genocide prevalent in history.

Consider what the Prophets says when the human rights are violated. *"the pleasant places of the wilderness are dried up, and their course is evil, and their force is not right." (Jeremiah 23:10)*.

(interlude—true witnesses)
Vision Three

(find in your Bible *these words* see Rev. 10:1–4)
mighty angel ~inspiration

Before getting to the third woe, there is an interlude. A *mighty angel* of justice, as if it were the sun, uncovers injustice. The mighty angel of justice is the fire that burns away the dross of injustice. The mighty angel of justice eradicates all mortal intelligence and substance and replaces them with immortal intelligence and substance.

The angel visitant puts forth the little book and a reed like unto a rod.

(find in your Bible *these words* see Rev. 10:5–11).
the little book ~guide

The mighty angel holds in open hand *the little book*. The command is to take it and *eat it up*.

Eat the spiritual import. Simply repeating or regurgitation the words of the Bible by themselves is benign, especially if one does not live by them. Whereas being filled with inspiration can sustain and guide one, even in the wilderness.

The bitter part typically is becoming aware of the huge divide between the interpretation of life from a material standpoint and the interpretation of life from spiritual being (see the parable of the great divide that separated by a great gulf the rich man from the poor Lazarus, Luke 16:19–31).

"Son of man, eat that thou findest; eat this roll, and go speak unto the house of Israel. So I opened my mouth, and he caused me to eat that roll. And he said unto me, Son of man, cause thy belly to eat, and fill thy bowels with this roll that I give thee. Then did I eat it; and it was in my mouth as honey for sweetness." (Ezekiel 3:1–3).

Some attribute this little book of prophecy to the Holy Ghost or Holy Spirit. *Thou must prophesy again.*

(interlude—false witnesses)
Vision Five

(find in your Bible *these words* see Rev. 16:13)
mouth of the dragon ~depression

Before getting to the third woe, there is an interlude. Instead of an angel, the *mouth of the dragon*. But be not dismayed. *"When thou art in tribulation, and all these things are come upon thee, even in the latter days, if thou turn to the LORD thy God, and shalt be obedient unto his voice; (For the LORD thy God is a merciful God;) he will not forsake thee, . . ." (Deuteronomy 4:30,31)*.

Counter-facts overcome the false trilogy—dragon, beast, and the false prophet. The merciless breeds its own downfall.

(find in your Bible *these words* see Rev. 16:13)
mouth of the beast ~misguide

Instead of a helpful book comes the *mouth of the beast*. It fails to guide. *"Take ye therefore good heed unto yourselves; . . . Lest ye corrupt yourselves, and make you a graven image, . . . The likeness of any beast . . ." (Deuteronomy 4:15, 16, 17)*. *"Shun profane and vain babblings: for they will increase unto more ungodliness." (II Timothy 2:16 shun)*. The spiritual sense of Scriptures, making each verse our own, growing in the understanding thereof, acting with our highest sense of selfless love, will never misguide.

(interlude—true witnesses)
Vision Three

(find in your Bible *these words* see Rev. 11:1, 2)
reed like unto a rod ~guard

The angel of justice, as a mighty king or as a humble shepherd, carries a rod for governing; *reed like unto a rod*. This rod is able to *rise, and measure*. The rod of justice helps direct the sheep. "*Feed thy people with thy rod, the flock of thine heritage,*" *(Micah 7:14)*.

This same rod of justice is also a woe to those in sheep's foe, those who enforce technicalities and dismiss morality. "*Then will I visit their transgression with the rod,*" *(Psalm 89:32)*.

Interfaith justice demands equality between neighbors—that none condemn in thought or deed any humble Jew, Christian, Muslim, or other tribe. Govern with grace to bring more harmony to daily experience. "*And I will cause you to pass under the rod, and I will bring you into the bond of the covenant (divine blessings):*" *(Ezekiel 20:37)*.

Some attribute this rod to Christ, "*And there shall come forth a rod out of the stem of Jesse, . . .*" *(Isaiah 11:1)*.

(find in your Bible *these words* see Rev. 11:3–14)
my two witnesses ~transform

Evil wars against *my two witnesses*, because they torment the ungodly. Yet the two great witnesses cannot be silenced. The Christ witnesses holy *phenomena* as the Holy Spirit witnesses holy *noumenon*.

The good and faithful may be crucified, but resurrection and ascension always follows. They are alive, *they ascended up to heaven*.

"*tribulation worketh patience; And patience, experience; and experience, hope: And hope maketh not ashamed; because the love of God is shed abroad in our hearts by the Holy Ghost . . . but we also joy in God through our Lord Jesus Christ, by whom we have now received the atonement.*" *(Romans 5:3–5, 11)*.

The interlude is finished. So *the second woe is past*. "*Thus saith the Lord God; Woe unto the foolish prophets, that follow their own spirit, and have seen nothing!*" *(Ezekiel 13:3)*.

(interlude—false witnesses)
Vision Five

(find in your Bible *these words* see Rev. 16:13)
mouth of the false prophet ~desertion

Instead of a rod comes the *mouth of the false prophet*. It fails to guard. "But there were false prophets also among the people, even as there shall be false teachers among you, who privily shall bring in damnable heresies, even denying the Lord that bought them, and bring upon themselves swift destruction. And many shall follow their pernicious ways; by reason of whom the way of truth shall be evil spoken of." (II Peter 2:1, 2).

Make a list of the ways the false prophet manipulates to give us a false sense of well-being. Now correct this to bring more harmony into everyday living. "Ye are my witnesses, saith the LORD, and my servant whom I have chosen: that ye may know and believe me, and understand that I am he: before me there was no God formed, neither shall there be after me." Isaiah 43:10).

(find in your Bible *these words* see Rev. 16:14–16)
Armageddon ~deform

Instead of resurrection, instead of humble witnesses serving the Holy Trinity, comes evil servants, the *spirits of devils, working miracles* of the unholy trinity of dragon, beast, and false prophet. The miracles lead to lust, personal selfhood, and doom. They do nothing to transform. Thus the war of wars, *Armageddon*. The false structure falls, like a *"house upon the sand"* (see Matthew 7:26).

The unlikeness of the Godhead being self-destroyed, the true witnesses make peace. The eternal fourfold structure is whole. "We have peace with God through our Lord Jesus Christ: . . . but we glory in tribulations also: knowing that tribulation worketh patience; And patience, experience; and experience, hope: And hope maketh not ashamed; because the love of God is shed abroad in our hearts by the Holy Ghost." (Romans 5:1, 3–5).

VII) Mercy without Justice is a woe
Vision Three

(find in your Bible *these words* see Rev. 11:15–18)
be judged . . . give reward ~Mercy & Justice

Now the third woe. Nations are angry. *Thy wrath is come.* Yet there is reward; *be judged . . . give reward.* "Blessed are they that keep judgment, and he that doeth righteousness at all times." *(Psalm 106:3).*

It sometimes appears that many which reap reward are cutthroats, betrayers, power mongers, etc. But this will not forever be true. *"Woe unto them that call evil good, and good evil; that put darkness for light, and light for darkness; that put bitter for sweet, and sweet for bitter!" (Isaiah 5:20).*

Those that obtain reward through evil means, will not maintain self-respect. Evil qualities gain unwanted reward—great woes. Contrarily, the Divine amply anoints and rewards with justice and mercy the prayerful servants in patient selfless love.

VII) Justice without Mercy is a plague
Vision Five

(find in your Bible *these words* see Rev. 16:17–21)
it is done ~Justice & Mercy

Now the third woe, *it is done*. Blessings that come from the merciful are as a great voice. Let us think, speak, and act with this heavenly voice.

Without mercy, punishment and wrath is exceedingly great. Justice without mercy comes to the disobedient evil qualities expressed by physicality, immorality, and wickedness in high places. *"He was a murderer from the beginning, and abode not in the truth, because there is no truth in him. When he speaketh a lie, he speaketh of his own: for he is a liar, and the father of it." (John 8:44).*

The woes of national disaster and global contagion are disturbing to human sense. It is disturbing because there is a belief that mankind is deficient or blameworthy, that those in need will not receive sufficient or timely recompense. Such state of existence should turn metaphysical thought toward a higher demonstration of neighborly love that can penetrate through corruption and political disorder.

Morally, no one should be without a calm trust that they shall always be cared for and lifted up. *"O Zion, that bringest good tidings, get thee up into the high mountain; O Jerusalem, that bringest good tidings, lift up thy voice with strength; lift it up, be not afraid; say unto the cities of Judah, Behold your God!" (Isaiah 40:9).*

(extension—Virgin)
Vision Three

(find in your Bible *these words* see Rev. 11:19, 12:1)
a woman ~Virgin

In vision three *a woman,* a virgin, appears. In vision five a harlot appears.

1. *clothed*
Vision Three

(find in your Bible *these words* see Rev. 12:2)
This virgin is *clothed with sun.*
Whereas the harlot is clothed in purple and scarlet.

2. *relationship*
Vision Three

(find in your Bible *these words* see Rev. 12:3)
This virgin's foe is *a great red dragon.*
Whereas the harlot's friend is the dragon.

(extension—Harlot)
Vision Five

(find in your Bible *these words* see Rev. 17:1, 2)
great whore ~Harlot

In vision five a *great whore*, a harlot, appears. In vision three a virgin appears.

1. *clothed*
Vision Five

(find in your Bible *these words* see Rev. 17:3–6)
A gaudy temptress, full of abominations.
Beware *purple and scarlet colour.*
What a contrast from being clothed by the sun.

2. *relationship*
Vision Five

(find in your Bible *these words* see Rev. 17:7–14)
The miasma is *of the woman, and of the beast.*
Those that express evil qualities, give their power
unto the beast and *make war with the Lamb.*
What will such friendship bring in the end?
Now reverse this.
Bring into the circle of friends
those that have uplifting motives and good works.

3. corona
Vision Three

(find in your Bible *these words* see Rev. 12:3)
The virgin exposes the dragon's false *seven crowns*.
Whereas the harlot desires the dragon's false authority.

4. habitation
Vision Three

(find in your Bible *these words* see Rev. 12:4)
The virgin exposes the dragon's motive, *to devour*.
But this will not happen.
Whereas the harlot's portion is full of violence and falls.

3. corona
Vision Five

(find in your Bible *these words* see Rev. 17:15–18)
False authority turns on oneself:
the *ten horns* which thou sawest upon the beast,
these *shall hate the whore,*
and *shall make her desolate and naked, and shall eat her flesh.*

4. habitation
Vision Five

(find in your Bible *these words* see Rev. 18:1, 2)
Babylon the great is fallen.
Fallen is the habitation of devilish evil qualities.
Abide in abominations and end up in a cage.
Angelic flight is given to the Virgin.
An impossible state for a harlot's state of mind.

5. ruling all nations
Vision Three

(find in your Bible *these words* see Rev. 12:4, 5)
This virgin's child to *rule all nations*.
including kings, including merchants
Whereas the harlot is fostering
warring nations, kings, merchants.

5. *ruling*
Vision Five

(find in your Bible *these words* see Rev. 18:3)
Mercy poured forth produces a holistic chemicalization,
cleansing toxic mental *fornication* and cancerous fear.
This mental rousing brings no harm to the holy.
It only dissolves the immoral compounds
in all *nations, kings,* and *merchants.*

5a. *all nations*
Vision Five

(find in your Bible *these words* see Rev. 18:4–8)
Come out of her, my people is the call from God.
For all nations shall see Harlot qualities burn,
burned with fire.

5b. *and the kings*
Vision Five

(find in your Bible *these words* see Rev. 18:9, 10)
And the kings of the earth shall see Harlot qualities burn,
smoke of her burning.

5c. *and the merchants*
Vision Five

(find in your Bible *these words* see Rev. 18:11–18)
And the merchants of the earth shall see Harlot qualities burn,
smoke of her burning.

6. protection
Vision Three

(find in your Bible *these words* see Rev. 12:5, 6)
This virgin dwells in *a place prepared of God*.
Whereas the harlot's place is destroyed.

7. sustain
Vision Three

(find in your Bible *these words* see Rev. 12:5, 6)
This virgin is continually sustained, *they should feed her*.
Whereas the harlot is sustained only one hour.

So ends vision three. Notice how vision three easily parallels vision five.

6. destruction
Vision Five

(find in your Bible *these words* see Rev. 18:19–21)
With violence shall that great city Babylon *be thrown down.*

7. abandon
Vision Five

(find in your Bible *these words* see Rev. 18:22–24)
All that belongs to the temptress shall be *heard no more.*
The harlot influence never was, is, or ever will be.
The harlot will not be sustained, not even of a third part.
The harlot has nothing to do with the virgin.
the voice of the bridegroom and of the bride
shall be heard no more at all in thee
These opposites are the tares and the wheat.

So ends vision five. Notice how vision five easily parallels vision three.

Vision Three
Summation

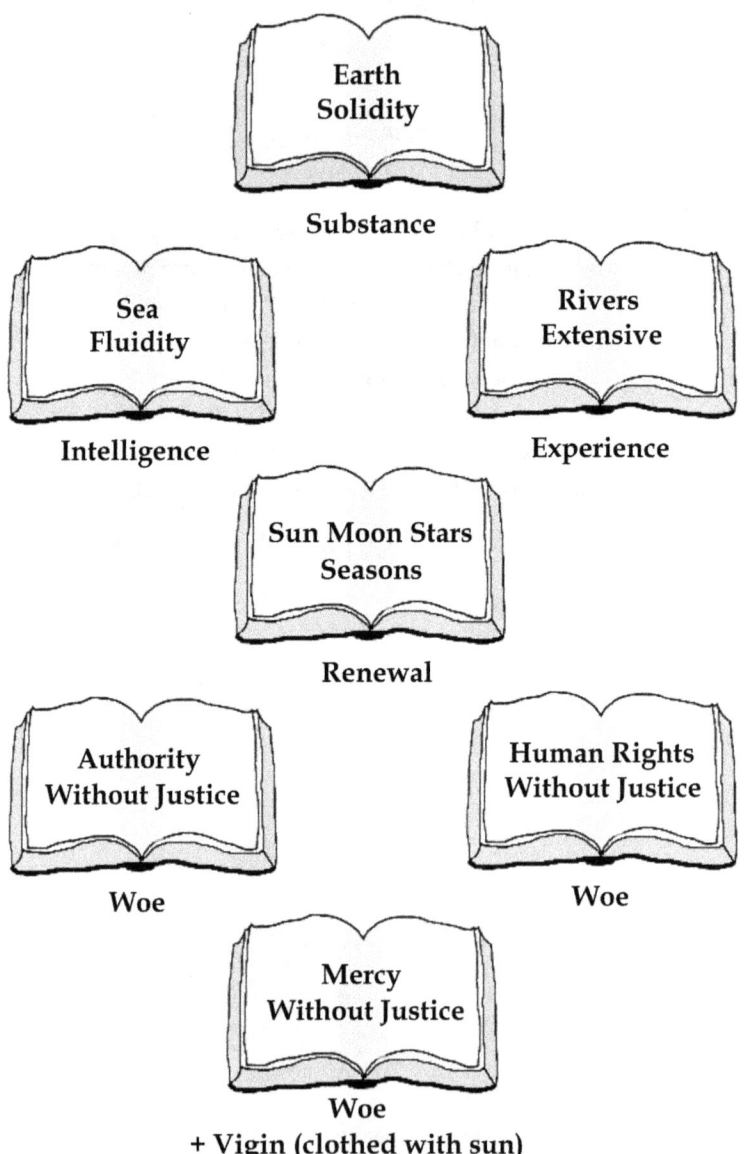

Vision Five
Summation

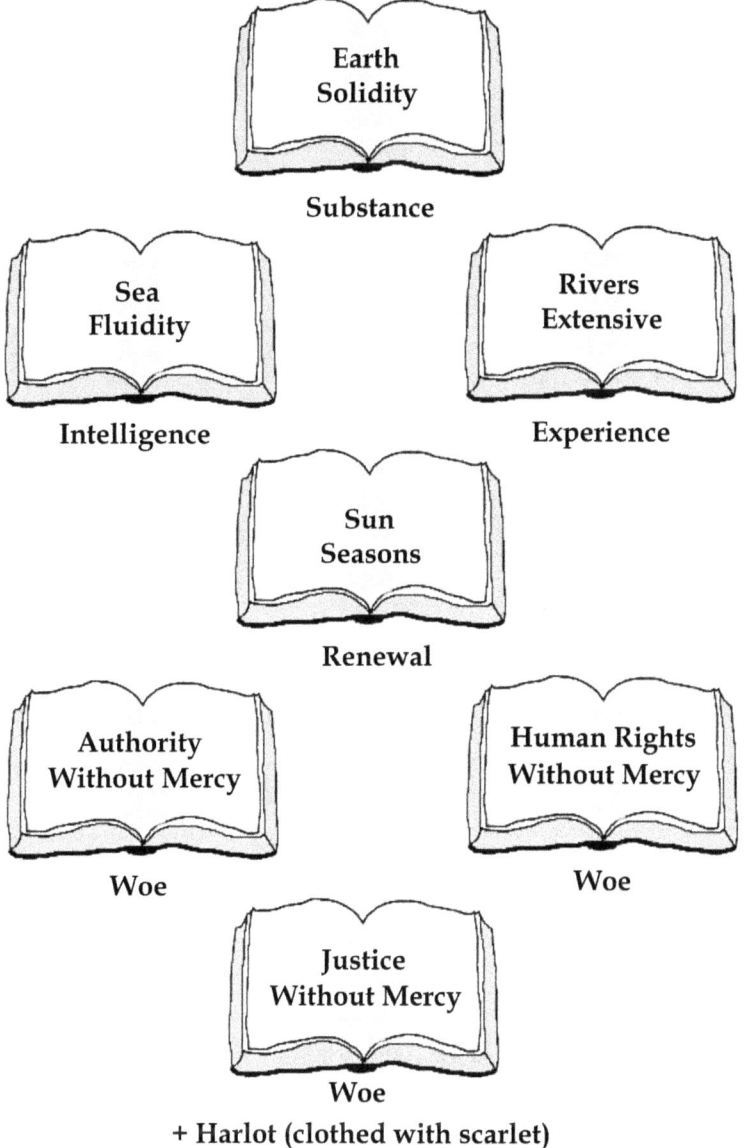

Vision Four

Preview

Dragon—Demonic Falsehoods

thou I walk through the valley . . . of death, I will fear no evil

(PSALM 23)

    I)   Evil is Temporal
    II)   Evil vs Virgin & Child
    III) Evil Pours (flood of despair)
    IV) Evil vs Remnant
    V)   Sea Beast, anti-Comforter
    VI) Earth Beast, anti-Christ
    VII) Mark of Sacrilegious

Central Key

for thou art with me thy rod & staff they comfort me.

(PSALM 23)

Father's Mark
New Song
Innocent Perfection

Divine—Angelic Truths

thou preparest a table before me in the presence of mine enemies

(PSALM 23)

    I)   Good is Everlasting
    II)   Good vs Harlot & Child
    III) Good Pours (wine of inspiration)
    IV) Good vs Remnant
    V)   Harvest Bread, Christ
    VI) Harvest Wine, Holy Spirit
    VII) Winepress of Communion

*Vision Four

Keystone (Rev. 12:7—14:20)

(find in your Bible *these words* see Rev. 12:7, 8)
war in heaven ~conscience

Over four thousand years ago Abraham spoke of only one God. Yet war on earth, and *war in heaven* between good and evil persists. Without good outweighing evil—social, economic, political, geographical, and religious wars will continue.

Fortunately the conflict of good and evil can cease, for in this *war in heaven: Michael and his angels* shall prevail over the *dragon and his angels*. Under God's grace, sooner or later thought shifts away from accepting mortality as a way of living. Conscience gleams with hope. Improving daily morality leads to enlightened consciousness. Then we understand it is not of us. We just need to yield to the will of God. Then behold the prophecy, the dragon angels *prevailed not*. "O thou enemy, destructions are come to a perpetual end: . . . the Lord shall endure for ever." (Psalm 91:6,7). Obedient to God's still small voice, we discover, *"the battle is not yours, but God's."* (II Chronicles 20:15).

The first chapter of Genesis explains a firmament separating evil from the good. Good is eternal, evil is temporal. Good is omnipotent, evil impotent. Thus the Seven Days explains the incorporeality of Creator, Creating, Creation, and the corporeality of wrong doing (the Adam & Eve story).

Note that scholars remark that the beginning chapter of Genesis amplifies the Latin phrase privatio boni. It means that evil, unlike good, is insubstantial; that evil is the absence or lack of good.

Vision four, the keystone, coincides with this privatio boni conclusion. The keystone of the archway to innocent perfection is spiritual consciousness, or experience containing only peace. *"For God is not the author of confusion, but of peace."* (I Corinthians 14:33).

The following pages expand this introduction by discussing: first the dragon and his angels (Dragon—demon messages); then the central theme of the Father's Mark, a New Song, and Innocent Perfection; then lastly Michael and his angels (Divine—angel messages).

The following pages provide a quick overview of vision four.

Dragon Demons
Vision Four

*thou I walk
through the valley
of the shadow of death,
I will fear no evil:*

(PSALM 23)

(find in your Bible *these words* see Rev. 12:9–12)
Dragon . . . and his angels . . . cast out ~prevail not

The keystone insures that the dragon and his messages prevail not; *Dragon . . . and his angels . . . cast out*. So, sooner or later all shall discover that evil, besides being forced to be silent, destroys itself, and thus has no place in heavenly consciousness. Dragon demon messages are nothing but lies about Elohim and the holy offspring. Evil traits attempt to cling to humanity, and by association we call such characters, imperfect and evil. However, through obedience or through suffering, all hypnotic qualities shall vanish. Thus all shall walk "through" the valley—and not stay or reside there forever.

The following describe seven demonic ideas that must not be accepted in consciousness, but rejected to bring more harmony to life.

Divine Angels

Vision Four

*thou preparest a table
before me in the presence
of mine enemies:*

(PSALM 23)

(find in your Bible *these words* see Rev. 14:6)
another angel . . . in the midst of heaven ~support unawares

These angel messages are not from the dragon, but from heaven divine; *another angel . . . in the midst of heaven*. Through obedience, or through enough suffering to purge disobedience, one arrives at the table prepared by Elohim. Having a morning meal at the edge of the Galilean sea, there is no fear. With repentant innocent perfection, outgrown lives are left behind. Enemies become only lost sheep to be brought back to the Shepard.

The transcendental is ever transforming. All partake of God's feast, and the three hidden measures of meal spoken of in the Bible raise spiritual being to a risen paradise.

Innocent perfection is not limited to only a few, but is available to all who sit at the holy table. *"be the children of your Father which is in heaven: for he maketh his sun to rise on the evil and on the good, and sendeth rain on the just and on the unjust."* (Matthew 5:45).

The following describe seven angelic messages entering consciousness with spiritual inspiration.

I) Dragon Temporal
Vision Four

(find in your Bible *these words* see Rev. 12:12)
knoweth that he hath but a short time

The inhabitants feel wrath—but only while maintaining evil thoughts and actions. Evil motives and deeds *knoweth that he hath but a short time.* Eradicate such and hold to inspired and grace-filled thinking and acting. Wrath cannot come down on enlightened consciousness. Corporeal earth-substance and sea-intelligence is a woe.

Ultimately, the false trinity shall be devastated, having but a short time. Soon after, dawns the virgin and her child in consciousness.

I) Gospel Everlasting
Vision Four

(find in your Bible *these words* see Rev. 14:6, 7)
everlasting gospel

The counter-fact to the demon message *"hath but a short time"* is that the divine message, an *everlasting gospel*. This is the idea presented by the first divine angel message.

II) Dragon Persecutes (virgin & child)
Vision Four

(find in your Bible *these words* see Rev. 12:13, 14)
persecuted the woman which brought forth the man child.

Persecution cannot affect the faithful and innocent. The persecuted are always afforded protection by God. Even the Dragon that *persecuted the woman which brought forth the man child.* cannot affect progress that unfolds grace. Hold fast to this fact, and see how it becomes reality. *"Blessed are they which are persecuted for righteousness' sake:" (Matthew 5:10).*

If depraved belief persecutes, lean not on one's own understanding, but silence fear so that one's inspiration can mount upon the wings of eagles. *"If I take the wings of the morning, . . . Even there shall thy hand lead me, and thy right hand shall hold me." (Psalm 139:9, 10).*

II) Self-Destruction (harlot & offspring)
Vision Four

(find in your Bible *these words* see Rev. 14:8)
Babylon is fallen

The counter-fact to the demon message *"he persecuted the woman which brought forth the man child"* is that the harlot's offspring, Babylon, is no more; *Babylon is fallen.* This wrath is self-inflicted, for nothing can ever successfully persecute the virgin and her babe of spiritual healing.

III) Dragon Pours (flood of despair)
Vision Four

(find in your Bible *these words* see Rev. 12:15, 16)
cast out of his mouth water as a flood

Seeming chaos, that *cast out of his mouth water as a flood,* cannot drown the faithful and innocent. The persecuted are always afforded life vests by God. Hold fast to this fact, and see how it becomes reality. "*Blessed are ye, when men shall revile you,*" *(Matthew 5:11)*.

If depraved belief persecutes, lean not on your own understanding but rise above the fear so that inspiration can place thee in the ark of safety.

III) Inspiration Pours (wine of inspiration)
Vision Four

(find in your Bible *these words* see Rev. 14:9–11)
wine, which is poured out

The counter-fact to the demon message that *"cast out of his mouth water as a flood"* is that *wine* of inspiration flooding evil, *which is poured out*. Divine messages filled with inspiration torments evil and its offspring of enigma. This wrath overflows with *fire and brimstone*, for evil thoughts and actions have no rest, day nor night.

IV) Dragon (wroth with servants)
Vision Four

(find in your Bible *these words* see Rev. 12:17)
war with the remnant

Thoughts of hate *war with the remnant*, yet those that undergo calamity, remain faithful. The servants of God keep the ten commandments of Moses and the testimony of the Lamb no matter temptation, persecution, or fear. These Old and New Testament commands of loving God, and loving your neighbor, are the everlasting covenant with the remnant who are full of grace and good deeds. *"And I will gather the remnant of my flock out of all countries whither I have driven them, and will bring them again to their folds; and they shall be fruitful and increase." (Jeremiah 23:3).*

IV) Remnant (blessed servants)
Vision Four

(find in your Bible *these words* see Rev. 14:12, 13)
patience of the saints

The counter-fact to the demon message that make "war with the remnant" *is* the divine message blessing the *patience of the saints*.

What do the remnant, the servants of God, and saint patiently keep? The commandments of God and the faith of Christly love. Often the Old Testament says "*keep the commandments.*" Often the New Testament mentions "*their works.*" Which is more needed, being thankful after it happens (gratitude), or being thankful before it happens (faith), *that they may rest from their labours.*

V) Beast of Sea (anti-Comforter)
Vision Four

(find in your Bible *these words* see Rev. 13:1–10)
a beast rise up out of the sea

A beast rise up out of the sea is the belief that intelligent life originated from inert fluid, and that a conscious brain eventually developed from primordial single cell bacteria. The sea beast is matter-produced intelligence. It is void of the Holy Spirit, Holy Ghost, or Comforter.

Mortal intelligence speaks with great corporeal-based scientific authority. Its physical laws dominate physical life. Its ten coronas attempt to nullify the Ten Commandments. The blasphemer offers physical healing through worshiping matter-based intelligence. But mortal understanding is not eternal, and only lasts a short time. Plus it has power only to those whose names are not written in the book of life.

The sea beast is the anti-Comforter *he opened his mouth in blasphemy against God*. The counter-fact is that the Holy Spirit is the true intelligence and science of divine health. *"Avoid the profane chatter and contradictions of what is falsely called science" (I Timothy 6:20).*

V) Harvest of Bread (Christ)
Vision Four

(find in your Bible *these words* see Rev. 14:14–16)
The harvest of the earth is ripe

The counter-fact to blasphemy against God or deception on earth is the fact that spiritual leaven is now present for the communion; *The harvest of the earth is ripe*. Here, bread is a symbol, the sustenance of good.

Partake of that spiritual bread. *"Wherefore do ye spend money for that which is not bread? and your labour for that which satisfieth not? hearken diligently unto me, and eat ye that which is good . . ." (Isaiah 55:2)*. *"Whereunto shall I liken the kingdom of God? It is like leaven, which a woman took and hid in three measures of meal, till the whole was leavened." (Luke 13:20, 21)*. *"I am that bread of life." (John 6:48)*

VI) Beast of Earth (anti-Christ)
Vision Four

(find in your Bible *these words* see Rev. 13:11–15)
another beast coming up out of the earth

Another beast coming up out of the earth is the belief that substance originated with earth-matter. The false prophet powers matter-based objects and science. It is void of spiritual form and science; the lamb, the way shower, the Christ.

The false prophet speaks with corporeal-based miracles. The blasphemer offers physical healing through worshiping the matter-based substance. Worldliness is full of its great wonders and pleasures, which mortals admire for they require no self-abnegation nor selflessness. Such material living allows no time for worshiping anything but the ego, which *deceiveth them that dwell on the earth*.

The beast of the earth is the anti-Christ. The counter-fact is that the Christ is the only true salvation for divine health. "*Mine heart within me is broken because of the prophets; . . . For both prophet and priest are profane; yea, in my house have I found their wickedness, saith the Lord.*" *(Jeremiah 23:9, 11)*.

VI) Harvest of Wine (Holy Spirit)
Vision Four

(find in your Bible *these words* see Rev. 14:17-19)
Her grapes are fully ripe

From the mental sea, the counter-fact to "blasphemy against God" or "deception from the sea" is the fact that spiritual wine is now present for the communion; *Her grapes are fully ripe*. Here, wine is a symbol for good. However wine can also be a symbol for evil. *". . . be not drunk with wine, wherein is excess; but be filled with the Spirit;"* (Ephesians 5:18).

Partake of that spiritual wine. "*For by one Spirit are we all baptized into one body, whether we be Jews or Gentiles, whether we be bond or free; and have been all made to drink into one Spirit." (I Corinthians 12:13)*.

VII) Mark of Sacrilegious
Vision Four

(find in your Bible *these words* see Rev. 13:16–18)
receive a mark

Much is written on the number *six hundred threescore and six* (666). Various interpretations abounds. Perhaps the disparities hint at a possible meaning, something "that cannot be explained". Amusingly, an enigma is something "that cannot be explained." Perhaps then this number representing evil is an enigma. Caution: enigmas tempt people to waste time in framing it.

I submit that those that *receive a mark*, are not human beings, but are traits of evil that try to mislead, such as: *"Adultery, fornication, uncleanness, lasciviousness, Idolatry, witchcraft, hatred, variance, emulations, wrath, strife, seditions, heresies, Envyings, murders, drunkenness, revellings, and such like:" (Galatians 5:19–21)*.

These enigmas, that try to attach themselves permanently to humans, can easily be dismissed. They have no power of themselves. Like mathematical errors, they only have power temporarily if someone thinks they are valid, and acts accordingly. Eventually the mistakes are found out, then rejected, and finally seen to be of no real importance.

Therefore avoid fearing (or even despising) mistakes, failures, as well as evil personalities. *"Now I beseech you, brethren, mark them which cause divisions and offences contrary to the doctrine which ye have learned; and avoid them." (Romans 16:17)*.

Fear not the mark of evil, those devilish traits that seem to be connected to individuals. The mark of evil is upon the trait, not upon the individual; as shown by Jesus Christ healing the insane (see Matthew 4:24; Matthew 17:15). Jesus Christ also healed plenty of sinners. Time and again he had compassion upon the suffering. His mission was not to fear but to bless and remove the mark of evil from the receptive and repentant.

VII) Winepress of Communion
Vision Four

(find in your Bible *these words* see Rev. 14:19, 20)
the great winepress

The pride of power, wealth, fame, etc. attempt to mark the way-shower. They try to crucify faithful with nails, a crown of thorns, and a spear. Yet this great squeeze from *the great winepress* of God, shall transform the purpose of a servant's sacrifice far outreaching any *horse bridles* (animalistic control), above any single period of history, and beyond any mortal sense of life.

Character traits, attributes, thoughts, and actions that have the mark of evil are all crushed and all life-blood that does not align with the great commandments will not be part of the communion, but be spilled outside the city (outside of the church consciousness).

There is no paradise for the disobedient who refuse to study, contemplation, and practice. Selfishness will be squeezed by suffering, until there appears at least a drop of gratitude and repentance.

"Greet one another with an holy kiss. The grace of the Lord Jesus Christ, and the love of God, and the communion of the Holy Ghost, be with you all. Amen." (II Corinthians 13:12, 14).

Central Key

for thou art with me;
thy rod and thy staff they comfort me.
(PSALM 23)

(find in your Bible *these words* see Rev. 14:1)
Lamb

The *Lamb* with justice and mercy comforts with Innocent Perfection. Now is revealed the very center of the arch of revelation.

"Behold, I and the children whom the Lord hath given me are for signs and for wonders in Israel from the Lord of hosts, which dwelleth in mount Zion." (Isaiah 8:18). Are not these children the followers of the Lord, the hundred forty [and] four thousand? Does this number include you? Yes. "Who then can be saved? . . . Jesus beheld them, and said unto them, With men this is impossible; but with God all things are possible." (Matthew 19:25). Innocent Perfection is our true state of being.

All are worthy to be a follower through repentance and spiritual baptism. Thus anyone can be worthy to receive the crown of glory. "*She shall give to thine head an ornament of grace: a crown of glory shall she deliver to thee.*" (Proverbs 4:9). "*And when the chief Shepherd shall appear, ye shall receive a crown of glory that fadeth not away.*" (I Peter 5:4). The crown of Innocent Perfection is in heavenly consciousness.

Faithful gratitude is a crown less worn than it should be. Complaint is the mouthpiece that sounds too often. Complaint is poverty. "*O ye saints of his, and give thanks at the remembrance of his holiness.*" (Psalm 30:4). In the divine economy of faithfulness, lack with all its false laws of supply and demand is null and void. "*by an equality, that now at this time your abundance may be a supply for their want, that their abundance also may be a supply for your want: that there may be equality:*" (II Corinthians 8:14). All are worthy, every day, to receive the *Lamb*, Innocent Perfection; as the next three sections explain.

Because thou hast made the Lord,
which is my refuge, even the most High, thy habitation;
There shall no evil befall thee

(PSALM 91)

Father's Mark
Central Key

(find in your Bible *these words* see Rev. 14:1)
Father's name written in their foreheads

Through the ages the forehead has been a sacred location, the seat of the mental realm; often used for colored stain, kissing, attaching a jewel, or bowing to the earth in humility. Now elevate the Father's mark or frontlet to the enlightened state. The *Father's name written in their foreheads* is eternal being. *"Mark the perfect man, and behold the upright: for the end of that man is peace" (Psalm 37:37).* Revelation is filled with differing names, and it is never too late to obtain the Father's mark and new name (like Saul changed to Paul). *"thou shalt be called by a new name, which the mouth of the Lord shall name." (Isaiah 62:2).* Listen. What new name does the *Father* give you for today?

The transformation of Jacob to Israel is a wonderful treatise. Likewise through Divine energy anyone can receive, or be marked with, a new regenerative identity. *"And be not conformed to this world: but be ye transformed by the renewing of your mind, that ye may prove what is that good, and acceptable, and perfect, will of God" (Romans 12:2).*

Rebirth, healing, and renewed character comes not with words or proclamations, but by seeing thy neighbor (and suppositional enemies—and even ourselves) in God's own image. Remember Jacob, he coveted, betrayed, and stole his brother's birthright. But through restitution and regeneration Jacob/Israel was able to say, *"I pray thee, if now I have found grace in thy sight, then receive my present at my hand: for therefore I have seen thy face, as though I had seen the face of God, and thou wast pleased with me." (Genesis 33:10):* Innocent Perfection.

Suffered and regenerated Job saw the face of God and was changed, marked as blessed, when he realized his salvation was not found by seeing himself as personally better or more righteous than another, but his salvation was found by including all as God's perfect offspring. *"I have heard of thee by the hearing of the ear: but now mine eye seeth thee . . . And the LORD turned the captivity of Job, when he prayed for his friends:" (Job 42:5, 10).* To obtain the Father's Mark, do likewise, pray for others!

New Song
Central Key

(find in your Bible these words see Rev. 14:2, 3)
new song

The musical chords of Spirit are: love, joy, peace, and a hundred more worthwhile qualities. These chords craft a *new song*. Sing, "Let there be peace on earth, and let it begin with me." *"Thy statutes have been my songs in the house of my pilgrimage." (Psalm 119:54).*

Interestingly Jesus Christ sang a song while on the cross. He sang a Psalm. Many may think it was a cry of anguish, *"My God, my God, why hast thou forsaken me?" (Matthew 27:46)*. However, any disciple can finish the song Jesus quoted from Psalm 22 in the Jewish Tanakh. Question: *"My God, my God, why hast thou forsaken me? . . . " (Psalm 22:2)* Answer: *". . . Our fathers trusted in thee: they trusted, and thou didst deliver them. They cried unto thee, and were delivered: they trusted in thee, and were not confounded." (Psalm 22:4, 5)*. One might sense the same essence from the Quran regarding Al-Qiyamah, where 75:1 begins with, "I swear by the Day of Resurrection."

The whole point of Jesus Christ's song is that trusting in God brings deliverance—a resurrection with an ascension. Jesus rejects suffering, because he healed the suffering. He upheld the melody on earth, healing the sheep not having a Shepard. With such compositions he rose himself and others from death. Another familiar Islamic song appearing numerous times is, *"which of the favours of your Lord would you deny?"* From the Tanakh, *"Hallelujah! For it is good to sing to our God; because He is pleasant, praise is fitting for Him." (Psalm 147:1).*

Jesus Christ taught all to compose their own salvation song, and to practice with holy notes of service. *"The LORD is my strength and song, and he is become my salvation:" (Exodus 15:2).*

Salvation, Innocent Perfection, Creator Creating Creation; sanctified through the Word, the Christ, the Holy Ghost, the Selfless-Love.

Innocent Perfection
Central Key

(find in your Bible *these words* see Rev. 14:4, 5)
without fault before the throne of God!

Having the Father's Mark, or spiritual identity, and a New Song, then all is good, all is innocent—without fault—perfect. *"Behold, I shew you a mystery; In a moment, in the twinkling of an eye," (I Corinthians 15:51, 52).* The mystery is revealed, Innocent Perfection is your spiritual state of being. Demonstrate this now, at least in part.

"Consider the incredible love that the Father has shown us in allowing us to be called 'children of God'—and that is not just what we are called, but what we are. Our heredity on the Godward side is no mere figure of speech—which explains why the world will no more recognise us than it recognised Christ . . . Here and now we are God's children. We don't know what we shall become in the future. We only know that, if reality were to break through, we should reflect his likeness, for we should see him as he really is!" (John 3:1,2 [J.B. Phillips]). Improve your atonement with the Supreme Being each day.

Always see others as without fault, as we would have God see us. *"Remember not the sins of my youth: according to thy mercy remember thou me for thy goodness' sake, O LORD." (Psalm 25:7).*

Being a servant without fault is likened to the Parable of the Dutiful Servant in Luke 10:7-10. *"Ye are my friends, if ye do whatsoever I command you. Henceforth I call you not servants; for the servant knoweth not what his lord doeth: but I have called you friends; for all things that I have heard of my Father I have made known unto you." (John 15:14, 15).*

Peace on earth is obtainable as we obey the two great commandments—loving God and loving our neighbor. Life does not have to include sin and suffering. Through the Divine insure that life includes more innocence and perfection.

Investigate Psalm 91 on a regular basis. The theme is consistent with the keystone: God's creation is Innocent Perfection, *without fault before the throne of God!* "He will make your innocence radiate like the dawn" (Psalm 37:6 NLT). *"let patience have her perfect work, that ye may be perfect and entire," (James 1:4).*

Vision Four

Summation

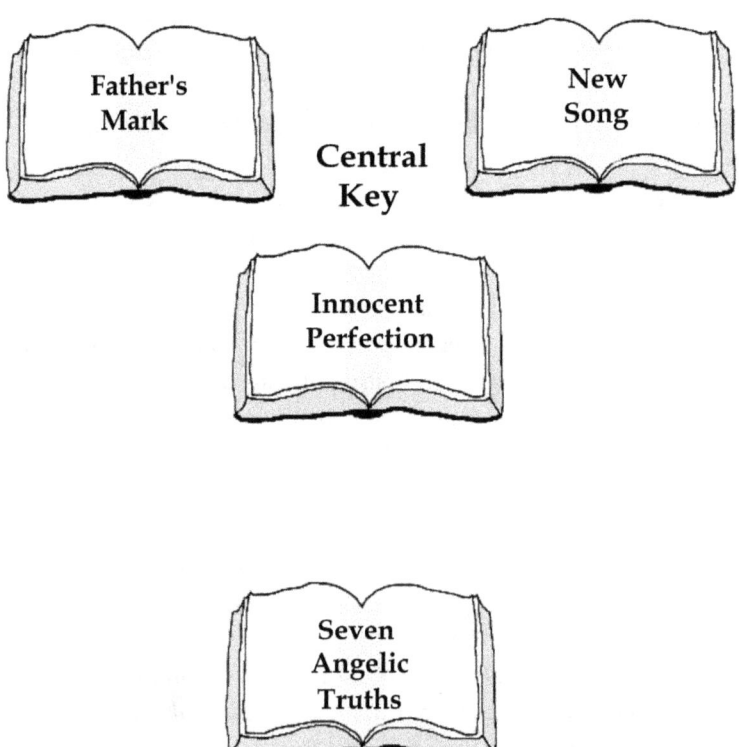

Revelation Conclusion

Hold on to the summary
of the Ten Commandments:

1–5) Understand God
(perfect God, good).
5–10) Demonstrate your Godlike childhood
(perfect offspring, good).

*"Be ye therefore perfect,
even as your Father
which is in heaven
is perfect."*
(MATTHEW 5:48)

Three parts follow
as Revelation concludes with:
Postlude, Epilogue, and Benediction.

Postlude (Rev. 22:3—22:5)

Revelation 22:2 ends with, *the leaves of the tree [were] for the healing of the nations.* "Verily, verily, I say unto you, He that believeth on me, the works that I do shall he do also; and greater works than these shall he do; because I go unto my Father." *(John 14:12).*

Think of papyrus as leaves written upon, and these leaves or healing messages parallel the letters to the seven churches discussed toward the beginning of Revelation.

I) Perfect Restoration
Curse removed, because God's children are found to be not fallen but upright. Likewise Ephesus worships discretion.

II) Perfect Reign
Persecution removed, because God's children are found to be faithful to the *throne of God*. Likewise Smyrna worships Fidelity.

III) Perfect Duty
Unrighteousness removed, because God's children are found to *serve* virtuously. Likewise Pergamos worships Righteousness.

IV) Perfect Identification
Self-indulgence removed, because God's children are *named* to be self-disciplined. Thus Thyatira worships Self-Control.

V) Perfect Presence
Unwatchfulness removed, because God's children are found to be attentive, with *no night there*. So Sardis worships Vigilance.

VI) Perfect Illumination
Partiality removed, because God's children are found to be equitable, as the *light of the sun*. So Philadelphia worships Impartiality.

VII) Perfect Eternity
Apathy removed, because God's children are found to be compassionate, *for ever and ever*. So Laodicea worships Empathy.

Epilogue (Rev. 22:6—22:15)

The epilogue answers the age old question, *"Master, which is the great commandment in the law? Jesus said unto him, Thou shalt love the Lord thy God with all thy heart, and with all thy soul, and with all thy mind. This is the first and great commandment. And the second is like unto it, Thou shalt love thy neighbour as thyself. On these two commandments hang all the law and the prophets." (Matthew 22:36-40).*

Interestingly whether faith comes from the Jewish Psalm of David, the Islamic Pillars of Mohammad, or the Christian Sermon on the Mount by Jesus Christ; all are the result of faith and hope in the Great Commandments that proceeded from the burning bush of the Divine. Let such burn in your heart each day of the year.

Blessed [are] they that do his commandments.

Benediction (Rev. 22:16—22:21)

The Book of Revelation is not to be added to, nor subtracted from. Meaning the inspired word is like the principle of mathematics. The principle of the divine exists, always has, always will. Like Alpha and Omega there is nothing to add or take away. If a new formula is discovered, or a new method like quantum physics is brought forth, it is nothing new to the universe (except to mere mortals). Eternal universal principles are all-in-all. *"it is the same God which worketh all in all." (I Corinthians 12:6).*

Discovery is progress. Progress is just finding out what already exists. The eternal is laden with yet an infinitude of undiscovered concepts. So discover as much as possible and find daily inspiration from the Book of Revelation.

The benediction will then follow, *grace . . . be with you all.*

Seven Visions

Summation

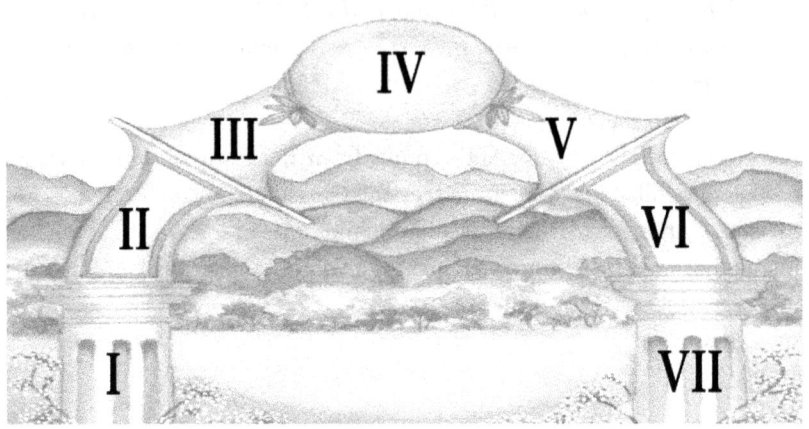

*Vision 4 (Rev 12:7—14:20)
Dragon Demons   Divine Angels
(temporal)   (eternal)
Innocent Perfection

*Vision 3 (Rev 8:2—12:6)   *Vision 5 (Rev 15:1—18:24)
Trumpets of Justice   Bowls of Mercy
(interludes)   (interludes)
Virgin extension   Harlot extension

*Vision 2 (Rev 6:1—8:1)   *Vision 6 (Rev 19:1—21:8)
Four Horsemen   Four Hallelujahs
three Woes   three Blessings
(goodness to servants)   (doom to evildoers)
Evil Silenced   Goodness Sung

*Vision 1 (Rev 4:1—5:14)   *Vision 7 (Rev 21:9—22:2)
Moses Tabernacle—Groom   Holy City—Bride
(Lord's Prayer)   (Seven Creation Days)
Worship Stations   Comfort Structures
(24 Sermons on Mount)   (24 Creation Concepts)

Seven Visions

Summation

Quintessence of Revelation from Palm 23:

*Vision 1   Fatherhood/Shepard
"The Lord is my shepherd; I shall not want."

*Vision 2   Calm Stillness
"He maketh me to lie down in green pastures:
he leadeth me beside the still waters."

*Vision 3   Justice
"He restoreth my soul: he leadeth me in the
paths of righteousness (justice) for his name's sake."

*Vision 4a
"Yea, though I walk through the valley
of the shadow of death, I will fear no evil:"

*Keystone: Innocent Perfection
"for thou art with me;
thy rod and thy staff they comfort me."

*Vision 4b
"Thou preparest a table before me
in the presence of mine enemies:."

*Vision 5   Mercy
"thou anointest my head with oil (mercy);
my cup runneth over."

*Vision 6   Goodness Sung
"surely goodness (justice) and mercy
shall follow me all the days of my life:"

*Vision 7   Motherhood/Comforter
"and I will dwell in the house (city) of the Lord for ever."

Matrix of Innocense & Perfection

biblical matrix
Interconnected—Inseparable
(and many more comparisons to be discovered . . .)

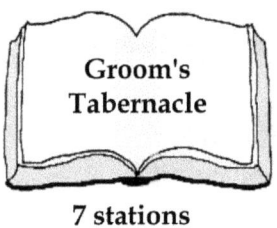

7 stations

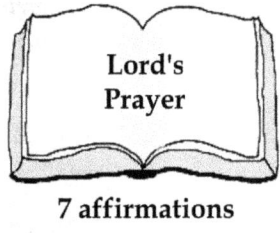

7 affirmations

7 formations

7 days

Author's Final Thought

Basically it is one's concept of Creator Creating Creation that determines one's experience. Therefore, hold fast to the Divine that is ONLY good. The opposite is a hypnotic suggestion of fear, followed by belief, which culminates into disobedience.

Unite with holiness by studying enlightened wisdom, followed by contemplating hints of the spiritual essence in nature, and in practicing grace and peace toward others. Be not like Adam & Eve, accepting the knowledge of both good & evil. Remember so long as corporeal character traits last, they are cursed and blocked from entering paradise.

Revelation's counter-facts swallow up evil and are victorious. Innocent identity, being of perfection, is a fact, the offspring of the Divine. Angelic thoughts bring comfort every moment as one improves in expressing the Word, Christ, Holy Spirit, and Selfless-Love.

If overwhelmed by worldly conditions: find a sliver of good in experience and be grateful. Thank God in discovering qualities of good (1st commandment). Help others discover qualities of good (2nd commandment). These are the purpose of life. *"He that loveth not knoweth not God; for God is love." (I John 4:8).*

Quickest way to grow in purpose: spend way less thought and activity in the corporeal realm; support the moral realm in acts of kindness, leaving the field to God for destroying evil; and endeavor to think and act from a sanctified standpoint.

Highlight favorite verses in Holy Writ. Don't bother with the harder to understand verses until they eventually become naturally clearer as one develops. Witness the infinite calculus of Bible Revelation, and note the Lord's Prayer aligning with the Seven Days of Genesis. Many are the marvels of supreme being.

One final thought that should make life more graceful and satisfying: *"seek ye out of the book of the Lord, and read: no one of these shall fail,"* (Isaiah 34:16).

www.ingramcontent.com/pod-product-compliance
Lightning Source LLC
Chambersburg PA
CBHW050824160426
43192CB00010B/1884